Unlocking SEO: Key Tactics for Digital Marketers to Boost Online Visibility V1

About

Ivan Bolfek is a seasoned SEO consultant hailing from Croatia, EU, with over 25 years of extensive experience in IT and search engine optimization. Renowned for his innovative strategies and deep understanding of the digital landscape, Ivan has dedicated his career to helping businesses enhance their online visibility and achieve sustainable growth. His wealth of knowledge and passion for SEO make him a trusted expert in the field, empowering digital marketers to unlock the full potential of their online presence.

Table of Contents

Intro

(1) - Here You Will Explore SEO and Effective White Hat Practices, Covering Everything From the Fundamentals to More Advanced Techniques

(2) - You Will Learn About Importance of Every Aspect of SEO, such as technical SEO, On Page SEO, and Off Page SEO, Also Known as Linkbuilding. Also, We Will Cover Other Advanced SEO Strategies, And beyond that

(3) - After Studying This Book, You Will Gain a Comprehensive Understanding of SEO and be Equipped to Apply This Knowledge to Optimize Real-Life Websites

Chapter 1: The Brief History of SEO

(1) - First search engines and their importance

(2) - When and how it started, SEO beginnings

(3) - Early SEO: The Rising Importance of SEO

(4) - When SEO became global business

Chapter 2: Understanding SEO Basics

(1) - What is SEO and Why Does it Matter?

(2) - Understanding Search Engines

(3) - The Importance of SEO for Businesses

(4) - Setting Realistic SEO Goals

(5) - Key Terminology Every Marketer Should Know

(6) - Components of SEO: Technical SEO, On-Page and Off-Page

(7) - Why Invest in SEO, Long Term Advantages Over Paid Marketing

Chapter 3: Setting Your SEO Goals

(1) - Identifying Your Business Objectives

(2) - Defining Measurable SEO Goals

(3) - Tracking Progress: KPIs to Watch

Chapter 4: Conducting Keyword Research

(1) - Understanding Keyword Intent: Navigational, Informational, and Transactional

(2) - Tools for Effective Keyword Research

(3) - Long-Tail vs. Short-Tail Keywords: Which to Choose?

Chapter 5: SEO and Content Creation Strategies

(1) - The Role of Quality Content in SEO, EEAT Framework

(2) - Building a Sustainable SEO Strategy

(3) - Balancing Short-Term Gains with Long-Term Growth

(4) - Incorporating Keywords Naturally in Your Content

(5) - Updating and Repurposing Existing Content

(6) - Creating an SEO Playbook

Chapter 6: Start With Technical SEO Fundamentals

(1) - The Significance of Site Speed

(2) - Mobile Optimization: Why It Matters Today

(3) - Ensuring a Secure Site with HTTPS

(4) - Setting up Google Search Console, Bing webmaster Tools, and Web Analytics

Chapter 12: Understanding Metrics and Pseudo Metrics in SEO

(1) - Google Metrics, Web Analytics and Other Pseudo Metrics Like Moz Explained

(2) - Analyzing Traffic Sources and User Behavior

(3) - Interpreting Rankings and Visibility Metrics

(4) - Conversion Tracking: From Click to Customer

(5) - Domain Authority (DA) and Page Authority (PA) MOZ Pseudo Metrics Explained and How it Can be Useful

Chapter 13: Keeping Up with SEO Trends

(1) - The Ever-Changing Landscape of SEO

(2) - Adapting to Algorithm Updates: What You Need to Know

(3) - Staying Ahead: Following Industry Experts

(4) - Continuous Learning and Adaptation

Chapter 14: Common SEO Mistakes to Avoid

(1) - Ignoring Mobile Users: Is it Really Mistake? What is Your Goal? Is it Low Quality Traffic?

(2) - Keyword Stuffing: Why It Backfires

(5) - Will AI Replace it All, or it Will Lead to New Golden Ages and a new beginning of Blogging and Content Creation

(6) - How Does Use of AI Has an Explosion of Potential, and a burst of possibilities

Conclusion: Get Free SEO Consultation

(1) - Contact us on Our Website and Get Free Consultation How to Improve Your SEO

(2) - We Have More Than 25 Years of Experience, and We Were Here Since Very SEO Beginnings

(3) - Importance of Good and Honest White Hat SEO Consulting, Reach Out to us For free Consultation Before You Start Your SEO Project

(4) - About Author: Ivan Bolfek, an Experienced SEO Consultant From Croatia

(5) - What do I do: Passionate SEO Professional About Sharing Valuable Insights and Information That Empower Others to Succeed Online

Intro

Here You Will Explore SEO and Effective White Hat Practices

Everything From the Fundamentals to More Advanced Techniques

SEO, or Search Engine Optimization, serves as a cornerstone of digital marketing. It's the art and science of improving your online visibility to attract organic traffic from search engines. Understanding the fundamentals of SEO is crucial for anyone looking to build a robust online presence. This includes grasping key concepts such as keywords, backlinks, site structure, and user experience. SEO isn't just about getting to the top of search results; it's about creating valuable content that answers user queries and meets their needs. When you optimize for search engines, you're also enhancing the user experience. It's a win-win. As webmasters and digital marketers, it's important to grasp how search engines function and what drives their algorithms, which change constantly. Keeping up with trends and updates helps us stay ahead in an ever-evolving digital marketplace.

White hat SEO practices refer to ethical strategies that align with search engine guidelines. These techniques are focused on delivering real value to users without resorting to manipulative practices that could lead to penalties. Emphasizing quality content is central to white hat SEO; this means writing informative, engaging, and relevant articles that address users' needs. Link building is another critical aspect, but it should be done organically by cultivating relationships and creating shareable content. When you engage in guest blogging or partnerships, it should be rooted in mutual benefits. Additionally, technical SEO elements such as mobile-friendliness, fast loading speeds, and structured data play a significant role in white hat tactics. By adhering to these principles, you can build trust with your audience and search engines alike, ensuring long-term success for your website.

A practical tip to enhance your SEO efforts is to always keep user intent in mind. When selecting keywords, think about what your audience is searching for and why. Use tools that help identify the questions people commonly ask related to your topic. By aligning your content with genuine user inquiries, you can improve engagement and retention, which are vital factors for SEO. As you implement these strategies, remember that patience and persistence are key elements in the SEO journey.

You Will Learn About Importance of Every Aspect of SEO, such as technical SEO, On Page SEO, and Off Page SEO

Also, We Will Cover Other Advanced SEO Strategies, And beyond that

Technical SEO is the backbone of any successful online presence. It ensures that search engines can easily understand and crawl your website. Think of it as the infrastructure of your site; it includes aspects like site speed, mobile-friendliness, secure connections, and proper indexing. Each of these factors plays a crucial role in determining how well your website performs in search rankings. If your technical SEO is lacking, all the content and backlinks in the world may not help you reach the top. On-page SEO complements this by focusing on the content itself and how it is structured. This includes utilizing the right keywords, optimizing title tags, crafting engaging meta descriptions, and ensuring internal links are used effectively. A well-optimized page not only appeals to search algorithms but also engages users, providing them with valuable information that keeps them on your site longer. Off-page SEO, commonly known as link building, amplifies your site's authority. It's about cultivating backlinks from reputable sites, which signals to search engines that your content is credible and relevant. The combination of these three aspects creates a solid SEO foundation that can significantly boost visibility and traffic.

Once you grasp the basics, diving into advanced strategies can truly set your site apart. Consider strategies like content clustering, where you create a hub page that links to various related articles, enhancing internal linking while providing a comprehensive resource for users. This not only helps with SEO but improves user experience, leading to longer site visits and lower bounce rates. Another advanced tactic is leveraging schema markup, which allows search engines to better understand the context of your content. By implementing structured data, you can enhance the way your site appears in search results, possibly yielding rich snippets that draw more clicks. Utilizing tools like Google Search Console and third-party analytics platforms can provide insights to refine your strategy and monitor performance effectively. Keep an eye on factors such as click-through rates, dwell time, and user behavior to refine your approach continuously. Staying updated on algorithm changes and industry trends will also keep your strategies relevant and effective.

Incorporating these advanced techniques can significantly enhance your SEO game. A practical tip to remember is to always put the user first. When crafting content or setting your SEO strategy, think about what will provide the most value to your audience. Engaging, informative content aligned with SEO practices not only fosters trust but can also lead to increased shares and backlinks, further amplifying your efforts. The landscape of SEO is ever-evolving, and embracing a user-centered approach will equip you to navigate this journey with confidence.

After Studying This Book, You Will Gain a Comprehensive Understanding of SEO

...and will be Equipped to Apply This Knowledge to Optimize Real-Life Websites

By the end of this book, you'll have a solid grasp of the essential SEO concepts that will empower you to effectively optimize websites. Understanding the core elements, such as keywords, meta tags, content quality, and link-building strategies, is crucial for driving traffic and improving search engine rankings. It's vital to recognize that SEO is not just a set of isolated tactics; rather, it forms a cohesive strategy that requires thoughtful integration. Armed with this knowledge, you'll be prepared to delve into hands-on applications of these techniques on real-life websites, bringing your learning to life and witnessing tangible results. You'll learn how to assess website performance, analyze competitors, and identify optimization opportunities that can set you apart in the digital landscape.

Building confidence in applying SEO tactics takes practice, but knowing the principles behind them can significantly ease any apprehensions. Start by experimenting with smaller projects or even your own website. This real-world application is where concepts turn into skills. Engaging with live data and seeing the results of your efforts will reinforce your learning and build your confidence. Participate in forums, seek feedback, and learn from other webmasters or digital marketeers. Don't be afraid to ask questions or test new ideas. SEO is always evolving, and staying curious will serve you well. Each small success will validate your skills and encourage you to tackle more significant challenges.

One practical tip as you begin applying what you've learned is to always keep your target audience in mind. Understand what they are searching for and tailor your content accordingly. The more aligned your content is with user intent, the better your chances of ranking higher in search engines. Conduct keyword research to uncover what terms are driving traffic in your niche and ensure those keywords find a place naturally within your content. Remember that SEO is about providing value, so prioritize user experience alongside optimization strategies.

Chapter 1: The Brief History of SEO

1.1 First search engines and their importance

Early search engines like Archie, Yahoo, and AltaVista fundamentally changed the way we retrieved information online. In those nascent days of the web, the vast expanse of information was overwhelming. Archie, which appeared in the early 1990s, was a simple tool that indexed FTP archives to help users find specific files. Yahoo, originally a directory structured by human curators, made it easier to browse through various categories and topics. These early platforms paved the way for a more sophisticated understanding of how to navigate digital content.

The importance of early search engines cannot be overstated. They acted as the bridges connecting users to the resources they sought, and their development highlighted the need for efficient information retrieval methods. As the internet grew exponentially, the limitations of having directories or basic indexing became evident, which led to innovations in algorithms and indexing methods. With the introduction of Google in the late 1990s, search engines began employing more advanced techniques like PageRank that revolutionized the way information was prioritized and displayed. This evolution transformed not only how users found content but also set the stage for the entire digital marketing landscape we now operate in.

As the online world expanded, the importance of search engines evolved dramatically. They became critical tools for marketers and businesses aiming to reach potential customers. Today, search engines are indispensable for finding information, shopping, and even entertainment. Their continuous evolution reflects an ongoing need to optimize for user experience, accessibility, and the relevance of content. For webmasters and SEO specialists, understanding how search engines have adapted and what drives their algorithms is essential for effective digital marketing strategies. Keeping up with these changes allows you to ensure your content stands out in an increasingly competitive space, enhancing visibility and engagement with your target audience. One practical tip is to routinely analyze your site's search performance metrics; they can provide invaluable insights that will help you align your efforts with search engine updates.

1.2 When and how it started, SEO beginnings

Search Engine Optimization, or SEO, has come a long way since the early days of the internet. Its roots can be traced back to the mid-1990s when the web started gaining traction among everyday users. At that time, search engines were simply tools to navigate the burgeoning digital landscape. They primarily relied on basic algorithms to index and retrieve content. The concept of SEO was born out of the necessity for webmasters to stand out in an increasingly crowded space. Understanding how search engines operated and how they ranked pages quickly became essential for anyone looking to drive traffic to their websites.

Foundational concepts like keywords and meta tags emerged as early SEO practices. Webmasters began to realize that by strategically placing relevant keywords in their content, they could increase the likelihood of their pages appearing in search results. Additionally, meta tags provided a way to communicate important information about a webpage to search engines, such as its title and description. These early adaptations laid the groundwork for what would eventually evolve into a more sophisticated and multifaceted field of digital marketing.

In the early days, webmasters undertook various methods to enhance their website visibility. Backlinking became a key strategy; webmasters would exchange links with other sites to boost their credibility in the eyes of search engines. The greater the number of links pointing to a site, the more authority it gained. This was a straightforward approach that yielded visible results, although it could be somewhat cumbersome to maintain. Selecting directories to submit sites also became a popular practice, as being listed in reputable directories could enhance visibility and drive traffic.

Keyword stuffing was another early approach—webmasters would load their web pages with keywords to manipulate rankings. However, this often backfired as search engines became more sophisticated and began penalizing such tactics. It wasn't long before SEO practitioners realized the importance of providing valuable, relevant content to not only attract visitors but also to keep them. This shift in focus to user experience began a transformation in SEO practices that prioritized quality over sheer keyword quantity.

Understanding these early practices is crucial for modern SEO specialists and digital marketers. Even as algorithms have evolved, the core principle of using relevant content to attract and engage users remains unchanged. By appreciating the journey of SEO, one can better navigate its intricacies today and adapt to the ongoing changes.

1.3 Early SEO: The Rising Importance of SEO

Understanding how SEO has transitioned from a niche concern into a necessity helps highlight its significance in today's digital landscape. In the early days of the internet, SEO felt more like a specialized skill set, often reserved for tech-savvy individuals and webmasters who had a deep understanding of algorithms and keyword strategies. The primary goal then was simply to drive traffic. However, as more businesses recognized the potential of the online marketplace, SEO evolved into a vital tool for visibility and competition. It became increasingly evident that having a website was not enough; companies needed a strategic approach to ensure their audience could find them amidst the overwhelming amount of content available online. This shift transformed SEO from an overlooked task into a crucial element of digital marketing that every business, regardless of size or industry, had to embrace.

The impact of SEO on the emerging online business landscape has been profound. As e-commerce grew and more brands launched their digital storefronts, the need for effective SEO strategies became paramount. Businesses began to realize that without proper optimization, no matter how innovative their products or services were, they would struggle to reach potential customers. Search engines became the primary gateways to the internet, and ranking well on these platforms meant the difference between thriving and merely surviving. SEO not only influences visibility but also enhances credibility; consumers tend to trust brands that appear on the first page of search results. Moreover, the evolving algorithms of search engines meant that businesses had to stay on their toes, regularly updating their strategies to align with best practices. This constant flux encouraged a culture of continuous learning and adaptation among webmasters and digital marketers, fostering a community focused on sharing insights and strategies.

As digital marketers and SEO specialists, it's crucial to remain aware of the trends shaping the future of SEO. The transition from a niche strategy to an essential component of business success teaches us that all companies, large or small, need to prioritize their digital presence. The focus on user experience, mobile optimization, and quality content is more important than ever. An effective tip for staying ahead in this ever-changing landscape is to invest time in understanding your audience and using analytics to guide your strategies. By doing so, you can ensure that your optimization efforts not only align with search engine algorithms but also resonate with your target market.

1.4 When SEO became global business

As I navigated the expansive world of digital marketing, it became clear that SEO was no longer just a strategy for businesses in developed countries. The global adoption of SEO by companies of all sizes and industries transformed the digital landscape. Small businesses in remote corners of the world started recognizing that a strong online presence could significantly influence their growth. With internet access expanding rapidly, countries that once had limited connectivity began using SEO to reach broader audiences. For instance, in places like Southeast Asia and Africa, local businesses began optimizing their content for search engines, allowing them to compete in the global marketplace. The advent of multilingual SEO further emphasized the need for localized content, making it possible for companies to cater to diverse audiences while maintaining their unique voice.

Several milestones marked the evolution of SEO into a significant industry. The launch of search engines like Google in the late 1990s catalyzed a frenzy of interest around website visibility. As search algorithms became more sophisticated, businesses began to understand the importance of keywords, backlinks, and user engagement. Conferences dedicated to SEO, like SMX and Pubcon, started appearing, serving as platforms where experts shared strategies and insights. The introduction of analytics tools also revolutionized the way businesses measured success. Suddenly, marketers had access to data that could highlight what worked and what didn't, enabling them to refine their strategies. Additionally, the rise of social media platforms and mobile optimization opened new avenues for SEO, further embedding it into the fabric of digital marketing.

As these developments took place, the perception of SEO shifted from a niche technical skill to a vital component of any business's growth strategy. The industry witnessed an influx of professionals eager to master the craft, leading to a burgeoning ecosystem of agencies, software, and educational resources. This meant that, regardless of geographical limitations, anyone could learn and apply effective SEO techniques. As I reflect on this journey, it's evident that staying updated with the latest trends and innovations in SEO is crucial. Embracing continuous learning will not only keep one competitive but also open doors to exciting opportunities in the ever-evolving digital landscape.

Chapter 2: Understanding SEO Basics

2.1 What is SEO and Why Does it Matter?

SEO, or Search Engine Optimization, is the practice of enhancing your website so that it ranks higher in search engine results. It's critical in digital marketing because it helps drive traffic to your site. When potential customers search for products or services that you offer, you want your website to appear at the top of those results. A well-optimized site is not only more visible, but it also attracts users who are looking for exactly what you provide. By optimizing various aspects of a website, such as its content, structure, and the way it interacts with other sites, you improve its chances of being found by search engines like Google. Major search engines use complex algorithms to determine what websites to display when users search for specific keywords. Therefore, caring for SEO means you are putting your best foot forward in the digital landscape, maximizing your chances of connecting with the right audience.

The benefits of SEO stretch far beyond just driving traffic. One of the most significant advantages is improved visibility, which leads to increased brand credibility. When your website ranks high on search engine results pages, it enhances your authority in the eyes of potential customers. They tend to trust results on the first page over those buried further down. Plus, a well-optimized website provides a great user experience, leading visitors to stay longer and explore more of what you offer. This not only enhances their perception of your brand but also tends to boost conversion rates. It's all interconnected; quality content that provides real value will naturally align better with SEO practices. Moreover, investing in SEO is a long-term strategy, which means the effects of your efforts will compound over time, delivering sustainable returns instead of just short-term spikes in traffic.

Understanding SEO is essential for anyone involved in digital marketing. It's not just about keywords anymore. We also need to pay attention to the user experience, like website speed and mobile-friendliness. Google values sites that provide a better experience for users, which in turn encourages responsibility and quality across the internet. A practical tip to enhance your SEO is to regularly update your content. Fresh and relevant content signals to search engines that your site is active, which can improve your rankings. Keep an eye on trends and incorporate them into your content to stay relevant. If you want to gain an edge, remember that SEO is an evolving field, and staying informed will only further your success.

2.2 Understanding Search Engines

Search engines are the backbone of online visibility. They are complex systems that retrieve data from the vast expanse of the internet, helping users find exactly what they are looking for with just a few keywords. The sheer volume of information available on the web makes search engines indispensable, and they play a crucial role in search engine optimization (SEO). Understanding how search engines work is vital for webmasters, digital marketers, and SEO specialists because mastering this knowledge allows you to create content that can effectively reach your target audience. The process begins when a user inputs a query. The search engine then scans its database for relevant pages. This operation relies on various algorithms that evaluate countless factors to determine which sites appear at the top of the search results. Therefore, if you want your site to stand out, it's essential to grasp how these systems function and their implications for optimizing your online presence.

Delving deeper, algorithms are the heart of search engines. They are sophisticated mathematical formulas designed to interpret users' queries and assess the relevance of web pages. These algorithms take into account a myriad of ranking factors, which can range from keyword usage, site speed, mobile-friendliness, to the quality of content and backlinks. Each search engine has its own set of criteria, and these can change frequently, which is why staying updated is crucial. As an SEO specialist, you'll want to analyze these algorithms and understand the ranking factors that influence your website's visibility. By doing so, you can tailor your content to meet these requirements and improve your chances of ranking higher in search results. Embracing this complexity might seem daunting, but it's the key to successful online marketing.

To enhance your understanding, always keep an eye on updates and shifts within search algorithms. One practical tip is to focus on creating valuable content that meets users' needs, as this remains a fundamental expectation of search engines. Prioritize the quality of your website's user experience and ensure that you are providing informative, engaging, and reliable content. This approach not only aligns with ranking factors but also builds trust with your audience, encouraging them to return. Remember, mastering SEO isn't just about technical tweaks; it's about understanding your users and delivering what they seek.

2.3 The Importance of SEO for Businesses

In today's digital age, having an effective SEO strategy is not just an option; it's a necessity for businesses wanting to thrive. Businesses of all sizes now compete in an online landscape filled with countless options for consumers. With more consumers turning to search engines for product and service recommendations, it's crucial that businesses are visible in search results. Without SEO, potential customers will struggle to find your website, which means missed opportunities and lost revenue. An effective SEO strategy not only boosts traffic to your site but also enhances brand credibility and customer trust. When a business ranks high in search engine results, it signals to customers that it's a reputable source. This is especially vital as consumers often gravitate towards the top results when making decisions. Implementing best practices for SEO can ensure that a website not only attracts visitors but also engages them, encouraging conversions and fostering customer loyalty.

Let's take a closer look at some case studies that illustrate the profound impact SEO can have on businesses. One notable example is a small online retailer that specialized in eco-friendly products. Initially, their website struggled to rank beyond the fifth page of search results despite offering quality merchandise. After investing in a comprehensive SEO strategy that included keyword optimization, quality backlinks, and regular content updates, the retailer saw their ranking climb to the first page. This improvement led to a staggering 300% increase in organic traffic within six months, and sales tripled as more customers became aware of their brand. Similarly, a local restaurant that was struggling to attract diners utilized local SEO techniques, such as optimizing their Google My Business profile and encouraging customer reviews. Within weeks, they noticed a significant uptick in online reservations and foot traffic, as diners searching for places to eat nearby could easily find them at the top of search results. These examples underscore how a tailored SEO strategy can deliver tangible results, from boosting visibility to enhancing customer engagement.

Understanding the value of SEO is just the first step; implementing it effectively can truly shape a business's future. For anyone involved in web management or digital marketing, focusing on SEO means not only keeping up with ever-evolving algorithms but also understanding user intent. The most successful SEO strategies reflect the needs of the audience, ensuring content is relevant and useful. Regularly updating content, conducting thorough keyword research, and analyzing performance metrics are vital practices that can lead to ongoing success. Always remember, SEO is not a one-time effort; it's a continuous journey that requires attention and adaptation. Embracing this mindset can help businesses not only compete but excel in the digital marketplace.

2.4 Setting Realistic SEO Goals

Articulating achievable SEO objectives is crucial for driving success. It's easy to get carried away with ambitious targets, especially when you see exemplary case studies or hear success stories from experts. However, it's vital to ground your objectives in reality. Start by analyzing your current situation. Look at your existing traffic, engagement metrics, and keyword rankings. Understanding these foundations helps you set goals that are not only aspirational but also practical. Break down your long-term vision into smaller, manageable milestones. For example, rather than aiming for a 100% increase in organic traffic within three months, consider a more gradual approach, like targeting a 20% increase over the next quarter. This way, you can celebrate small victories while remaining focused on your ultimate goals.

Aligning your SEO goals with your overall business strategy is essential for cohesive growth. Every marketing effort you undertake should dovetail with your company's broader objectives. Start by engaging with different teams—like sales, customer service, and product development—to understand their goals and challenges. This collaborative approach allows you to craft SEO goals that support and enhance these wider business objectives. For instance, if your company aims to improve customer retention, you can set SEO targets that involve creating valuable content geared towards existing customers, enhancing user experience, and addressing common concerns. By ensuring that your SEO aims are not isolated but rather a part of the holistic strategy, you pave the way for a synergistic effect that maximizes impact.

Setting realistic SEO goals is an ongoing process. Don't forget to revisit and adjust your objectives based on performance analytics and market changes. Regularly reviewing and recalibrating your goals keeps you on track and allows you to pivot when necessary. A useful practical tip is to establish a quarterly review system. During these reviews, evaluate what's working and what isn't, and make data-driven adjustments. This flexible approach helps maintain momentum and ensures that your SEO efforts remain relevant and effective, allowing you to continuously align with both your tactical and strategic business needs.

2.5 Key Terminology Every Marketer Should Know

Search Engine Optimization, or SEO, has its own unique language that can sometimes feel overwhelming. Terms like backlink, keyword density, and meta tags float around in conversations, often leaving those unfamiliar with them in the dust. A backlink refers to any incoming link from another website to yours and is crucial because search engines view them as endorsements of your content. The more quality backlinks you have, the more likely your site will rank higher on search results. Keyword density, on the other hand, is a measure of how often keywords appear in your content compared to the total word count. Finding the right balance is essential; too few may signal to search engines that your content is irrelevant, while too many can be viewed as spammy. Meta tags are snippets of text that describe a page's content; they don't appear on the page itself but in the page's source code, influencing how search engines understand and categorize your web pages.

Creating a glossary of terms can provide immense value, especially for those diving headfirst into SEO discussions. Understanding each term can enhance communication and strategy formulation among webmasters and digital marketers. For instance, terms like page authority and domain authority help you gauge the strength of your website, while bounce rate gives insights into user engagement and experience. Knowing these terms means you can discuss site performance and improvements intelligently. Grasping the differences between organic and paid search results is equally vital; organic search results appear naturally due to their quality of content, whereas paid results are boosted through advertising. Familiarizing yourself with these phrases lays the groundwork for deeper, more fruitful conversations about strategies and tactics in the realm of SEO.

One key takeaway is the importance of staying updated on SEO terminology as the landscape involves constant changes. New terms and concepts emerge regularly with shifts in algorithms and user behavior. Making it a habit to regularly refresh your knowledge can significantly impact your marketing strategies. Consider joining SEO forums or subscribing to newsletters to stay up to speed. By doing so, you'll not only enhance your own understanding but also contribute meaningfully to discussions with fellow specialists.

2.6 Components of SEO: Technical SEO, On-Page and Off-Page

Understanding the components of SEO is crucial for anyone involved in digital marketing. SEO, or Search Engine Optimization, can be broken down into three primary components: technical SEO, on-page SEO, and off-page SEO. Each of these components plays a vital role in improving a website's visibility on search engines. Technical SEO focuses on the backend aspects of a website. This includes site speed, mobile-friendliness, indexing, and crawlability. It ensures that search engines can easily access and navigate your site. On-page SEO, on the other hand, pertains to the content and layout of your pages. It revolves around optimizing titles, headings, and meta descriptions while ensuring that content is valuable and relevant. Finally, off-page SEO involves external elements, particularly backlinks and social signals, that affect your site's credibility and authority. Together, these components form a holistic approach to optimization.

The synergy between technical, on-page, and off-page SEO is what leads to effective optimization. Think of it like a well-oiled machine; if one part isn't functioning correctly, it can hinder the overall performance. For example, if your technical SEO isn't set up to support indexing, even the best on-page content may not get ranked effectively. Conversely, if you have a technically sound site and great page content, but lack quality backlinks, you may struggle to achieve higher rankings. Each component supports and enhances the others, creating a ripple effect that can either improve or harm your site's visibility in search results. Therefore, it's essential to consider all three aspects comprehensively. Regular audits of your site can help identify areas where you may need to focus your efforts more.

In practical terms, if you're looking to boost your website's performance, start by ensuring your technical SEO basics are covered. Use tools like Google Search Console to check for crawl errors, and make sure your site is mobile-responsive. Then, move on to optimizing your content with relevant keywords and engaging formats to captivate your audience. Lastly, don't overlook the importance of building a robust backlink profile through guest blogging, partnerships, and social interactions. By harmonizing these three aspects, you'll pave your way to better search engine rankings and a more successful online presence.

2.7 Why Invest in SEO, Long Term Advantages Over Paid Marketing

Investing in SEO can be one of the smartest long-term marketing moves you can make. Unlike paid marketing, which can provide immediate but often short-lived results, SEO builds a solid foundation for ongoing traffic and visibility. Once your website earns a strong ranking on search engines, it can continue to attract organic traffic without the constant flow of funds that paid ads require. This is particularly important in a digital landscape where users tend to trust organic search results more than paid advertisements, making SEO a pathway to increased credibility and authority in your niche.

Moreover, good SEO practices not only optimize your site for search engines but also enhance user experience. A site that loads quickly, is mobile-friendly, and provides valuable content will naturally engage visitors longer, reducing bounce rates and increasing conversion rates. That's the beauty of SEO—while the initial investment of time and resources may seem daunting, the ongoing benefits can significantly outweigh them. With diligent effort, your content can sustain its value over time, attracting new viewers long after it was published. This cumulative growth in traffic and engagement reinforces your brand presence and can lead to higher trust levels among your audience.

When you think about marketing strategies, paid ads and SEO are two prominent approaches, yet they have distinct characteristics that make them suitable for different goals. Paid marketing offers instant visibility and can be a great way to generate traffic quickly, especially for time-sensitive promotions. However, this visibility often hinges on your advertising budget—once you stop paying, the traffic can drop off dramatically. In contrast, SEO is a marathon, not a sprint. While it may take some time to climb the ranks on search engines, the traffic you gain is often more consistent and reliable in the long run.

Another factor to consider is the cost. Paid marketing can be quite expensive, with costs mounting for each click or impression. SEO requires a different type of investment, usually in terms of time and expertise rather than hard cash. Once your content is ranking well, it can continue to drive traffic without additional costs, making it an economically savvy option over time. The relationship between SEO and content is also significant; high-quality, relevant content fuels both good SEO and effective paid campaigns. By investing in strong SEO foundations, you also improve the effectiveness of any paid marketing efforts you may pursue in the future.

Understanding the dynamics between SEO and paid marketing can help guide your strategy. A balanced approach often brings the best of both worlds. Use paid marketing for immediate visibility and crucial short-term campaigns, while simultaneously building your SEO efforts for lasting results. This synergy can lead to an optimized digital presence that works for your business in a flexible and sustainable manner.

Chapter 3: Setting Your SEO Goals

3.1 Identifying Your Business Objectives

Aligning SEO goals with business objectives is crucial for any webmaster or digital marketer. When SEO strategies are in sync with the broader vision of the business, achieving results becomes much simpler. For example, if the main business objective is to increase revenue through online sales, the SEO goals should focus on driving targeted traffic to product pages and improving their rankings on search engines. This alignment not only helps in maximizing the return on investment but also guides the decisions made along the way. It ensures that every SEO tactic is purposeful and directed towards contributing to the larger business goals, rather than chasing metrics that may not have a direct effect on revenue growth or brand awareness.

Identifying your core business objectives can seem daunting, but there are various tools and methods that can make this task easier. One effective approach is to conduct a SWOT analysis, focusing on strengths, weaknesses, opportunities, and threats. This helps in evaluating where your business stands and what direction it should pursue. Additionally, tools like Google Analytics can provide valuable insights into visitor behavior, allowing you to understand what resonates with your audience and how they interact with your website. Surveys and customer feedback can also highlight what your customers value most, informing your business strategy. Using these insights, you can craft specific and measurable objectives that not only support your SEO efforts but also propel your entire business forward.

A practical tip to remember is to always revisit and adjust your objectives regularly as the digital landscape is constantly changing. Staying flexible allows you to adapt your SEO strategies and keep them aligned with evolving business goals.

3.2 Defining Measurable SEO Goals

Setting specific and measurable SEO goals is essential for tracking your website's performance. You want to have clear targets that help you gauge progress, rather than vague objectives that can lead to confusion. For instance, instead of saying I want more traffic, a specific goal would be I want to increase organic traffic by 30% over the next six months. This particular goal not only outlines the desired outcome but also sets a timeframe, allowing for focused efforts and assessments along the way. When you articulate your goals clearly, you can align your SEO strategies to those objectives, whether it's targeting specific keywords, increasing your domain authority, or improving conversion rates.

As you define these objectives, consider the aspects of your website that contribute to overall performance. Maybe you want to improve your website's loading speed, enhance user experience, or target a new audience segment. By choosing measurable goals, you will not only foster accountability but can also celebrate the small wins that lead to the bigger picture. For example, you can track important milestones like achieving a certain number of backlinks or improving your rankings for specific keywords. This continuous tracking allows you to adjust your strategies as necessary, ensuring that you are always moving in the right direction.

Key performance indicators (KPIs) are fundamental when it comes to measuring the success of your SEO efforts. By incorporating relevant KPIs into your goal-setting process, you create a bridge between your objectives and tangible data. For instance, if your goal is to enhance visibility, you might track rankings for specific keywords, as well as organic click-through rates. These metrics provide valuable insights, helping you understand how well your strategies are working and where adjustments may be needed.

Different KPIs will resonate depending on your unique objectives. If you're focused on driving conversions, you might look at metrics like conversion rate from organic traffic or the number of leads generated. Alternatively, if brand awareness is your focus, tracking social shares or branded search volume can provide clarity on how well your SEO efforts are impacting your audience perception. Whatever your goals may be, remember that the key to effective tracking lies in selecting KPIs that mirror your defined objectives. Tailoring your approach in this way allows you to make data-driven decisions, ensuring that every action you take moves you closer to your goals. To stay ahead, regularly revisit and refine your KPIs; this practice will keep them inline with any shifts in your strategy and overall business objectives.

As you set out to define your measurable SEO goals, make a habit of linking each goal to specific KPIs. This practical approach will enhance your ability to diagnose issues, identify opportunities, and celebrate achievements along your SEO journey.

3.3 Tracking Progress: KPIs to Watch

When we think about SEO success, there are several key performance indicators (KPIs) that we simply cannot overlook. Organic traffic is often the first KPI that comes to mind. It shows the number of visitors arriving at your site through search engine results without any paid advertising. Tracking this number over time helps us understand whether our SEO efforts are paying off. Another vital KPI is the keyword rankings. By monitoring the positions of target keywords in search engines, we can see how well our content is performing and whether adjustments are needed to stay competitive in our niche. Additionally, we should pay attention to the click-through rate (CTR) for our search listings. A high CTR indicates that users find our title and meta description compelling, which encourages more clicks and potentially higher rankings over time.

Engagement metrics, such as bounce rate and average session duration, also provide insights into SEO success. A high bounce rate might indicate that visitors are not finding what they were looking for on our pages, which could be a red flag for both user experience and SEO. Conversely, a longer average session duration typically means that users are interacting with our content, which is a positive sign for search engines. Furthermore, monitoring conversions from organic traffic is crucial. This tells us whether those visitors are taking desired actions on our website, such as filling out forms or making purchases. Lastly, keeping an eye on backlinks is essential. The number and quality of backlinks can significantly influence our site's authority and search rankings.

Understanding the results of our KPIs is just as important as tracking them. Once we've gathered enough data, it's time to analyze what those numbers actually mean for our SEO strategy. For instance, if we notice a steady increase in organic traffic but a low conversion rate, we might need to take a closer look at our landing pages. Are they designed effectively to turn visitors into customers? This could be a sign that while our traffic is growing, the content or design might not be enticing enough to retain visitors and prompt action.

Interpreting keyword rankings requires a slightly different approach. If we see fluctuations in our rankings, we should assess potential causes—perhaps there has been a Google algorithm update, or we may have fallen behind in content creation or optimization. By staying on top of industry trends and regularly updating our content according to keyword performance, we can adjust our strategy accordingly. It's also useful to set benchmarks or goals for each KPI. This allows us to quickly recognize deviations from expected performance so we can take corrective action. For instance, if our bounce rate suddenly rises, we can investigate the affected pages and make necessary adjustments to enhance user experience.

In planning our next steps, consider A/B testing as a valuable tool. By experimenting with different title tags or meta descriptions, we can determine what resonates best with our audience, helping to improve our CTR. And remember, SEO is an ongoing process. Regular review and adjustments based on KPI outcomes will ensure that our strategies remain effective and aligned with our business goals and audience needs.

Chapter 4: Conducting Keyword Research

4.1 Understanding Keyword Intent: Navigational, Informational, and Transactional

Keyword intent can be categorized into three main types: navigational, informational, and transactional. Each type plays a crucial role in understanding what users are looking for when they conduct a search. Navigational intent refers to searches where users are trying to get to a specific website or page. For instance, someone searching for Facebook login is likely aiming to access their Facebook account directly. Recognizing this type of intent helps webmasters tailor their site's structure and navigation to ensure that users can easily find what they need when visiting their site.

Informational intent, on the other hand, encompasses searches where users seek knowledge or answers to specific questions. This could range from how to bake a chocolate cake to what is the capital of France. Understanding this intent is vital for content creators who want to establish authority and provide valuable information. By analyzing common questions or topics relevant to your audience, you can create blog posts, guides, or FAQs that match their queries, ultimately driving more traffic to your site.

Transactional intent signals that users are ready to make a purchase or take some kind of action, like buy Nike shoes online or subscribe to premium service. When you know that users are in a buying mindset, your content strategy can focus on conversion elements like clear calls-to-action, product comparisons, and promotional offers. It's about meeting users where they are in their journey and providing them with the information they need to make informed decisions. A useful tip is to constantly analyze the terms that lead to your product pages and adjust your content accordingly to highlight the right messaging that speaks to users at that critical moment of decision.

4.2 Tools for Effective Keyword Research

Numerous keyword research tools are available to marketers today, each offering unique features and benefits tailored to different aspects of search engine optimization. At the forefront, we find tools like Google Keyword Planner, which provides insights directly from the search ads ecosystem, giving a glimpse into what users are actively searching for. SEMrush is another powerhouse; it not only highlights keyword opportunities but also offers competitive analysis, letting you see what your rivals are targeting. Moz's Keyword Explorer is known for its intuitive interface and rich analytics, allowing for a deeper understanding of keyword difficulty and potential traffic. Ubersuggest, a favorite among cost-conscious marketers, provides comprehensive keyword data and suggestions with an easy-to-navigate layout. Each of these tools brings something valuable to the table, and learning how to use them effectively can make a significant difference in your SEO strategy.

To leverage these tools for actionable insights, it's essential to dive deeper than just surface-level data. Start by defining your target audience and their potential search behaviors. With this clarity, input relevant seed keywords into your chosen tool to explore variations that might resonate with your audience. Pay close attention to metrics like search volume, keyword difficulty, and trends over time.

It's not just about finding popular keywords; it's about identifying phrases that match user intent and align with your content strategy. Consider using long-tail keywords, as they often yield higher conversion rates since they are more specific and less competitive. Once you gather a comprehensive list of keywords, categorize them based on your content themes or product offerings. This organization helps in strategizing your content creation efforts, ensuring each piece serves a particular purpose and targets the right keyword effectively.

Ultimately, continuous monitoring and adjusting of your keyword strategy is key. Regularly revisit your chosen tools to track how your keywords perform over time and how market trends may be shifting. Always be ready to adapt as new data comes in. The digital landscape is constantly evolving, and being proactive will keep your approach fresh and relevant. A practical tip is to set aside time each month to review your keyword performance and adjust your content plans accordingly. This will not only sharpen your SEO tactics but also keep you in tune with what your audience is looking for.

4.3 Long-Tail vs. Short-Tail Keywords: Which to Choose?

Keywords are essential in digital marketing and search engine optimization. They are the phrases that users enter into search engines to find information, products, or services. Short-tail keywords are typically one or two words long and are broad in nature. An example would be shoes or digital marketing. These keywords often have high search volumes but can be incredibly competitive, making it harder to rank high in search results. On the other hand, long-tail keywords consist of three or more words and are more specific. For instance, best running shoes for flat feet or how to create an effective digital marketing strategy are long-tail keywords. While they generate lower search volumes compared to short-tail keywords, they usually result in better engagement and conversion rates because they often reflect more targeted user intent.

Understanding the application of both types of keywords is crucial. Short-tail keywords can help to drive a larger amount of traffic to your site, but that traffic might be less relevant. Long-tail keywords cater to a more specific audience willing to engage more meaningfully. Incorporating both types into your content strategy can help you reach a broader audience while still attracting those who are ready to take action.

Each type of keyword comes with its own set of advantages and disadvantages. Short-tail keywords can boost overall website traffic quickly, allowing for rapid visibility. However, their competitiveness means that achieving top rankings can be more challenging and often requires more extensive resources. A disadvantage is that the visitors attracted by short-tail keywords may not convert into customers due to a mismatch in intent. Long-tail keywords, while generating less traffic, often yield a higher conversion rate since they reflect a more refined search intent. The downside is that you might miss out on broader exposure due to the lower volume of searches they attract.

Incorporating these keywords into your digital marketing strategy involves a balanced approach. Start by targeting short-tail keywords to establish a foundation and visibility in search engines. As your website gains authority, you can shift focus to integrating long-tail keywords. Utilizing tools like Google Keyword Planner or SEMrush can help you identify keywords that align with your niche. A practical tip to boost your strategy is to create content that answers specific questions, as people increasingly use voice search to ask detailed queries. This way, you can naturally weave long-tail keywords into your content while crafting highly relevant, engaging articles or blog posts that appeal to your target audience.

Chapter 5: SEO and Content Creation Strategies

5.1 The Role of Quality Content in SEO, EEAT Framework

The EEAT framework, which stands for Expertise, Authoritativeness, and Trustworthiness, is becoming increasingly vital in the realm of SEO. This framework plays a crucial role in how content is perceived by both users and search engines. When you think about SEO, the quality of your content directly influences your search rankings. High-ranking websites typically exhibit a strong EEAT, which helps them appear credible and reliable in the eyes of search engines like Google. By focusing on EEAT, we can craft content that not only connects with our audience but also earns the favor of search algorithms. Understanding this relationship is key for webmasters and digital marketers aiming to enhance their online presence. Referring to this framework assists in developing a strategic approach toward creating content that resonates, ensuring it meets the high standards set by search engines.

An essential part of producing quality content lies in its ability to enhance SEO performance. Quality content should not only be informative but also engaging and relevant to the target audience. Factors like keyword optimization, which involves using the right terms without keyword stuffing, play an important role. Moreover, incorporating rich, comprehensive information can boost your content's authority and trustworthiness. Quality content also comes with a unique voice and perspective that stands out, making it easy for readers to connect with it deeply. This engagement leads to higher user retention and lower bounce rates, contributing positively to SEO metrics. Placing emphasis on creating substantial, well-researched articles that answer real questions or solve problems helps build expertise. Supporting claims with data, references, and proper citation fosters trust among users. When crafting quality content, it's also important to ensure that it is easily digestible, utilizing headings, bullet points, and visuals where appropriate. This type of content not only attracts the right audience but also encourages users to share it, which in turn amplifies organic reach.

5.2 Building a Sustainable SEO Strategy

Building a sustainable SEO strategy is about creating a framework that can withstand the changing tides of the digital landscape. It starts with a thorough understanding of your audience and their needs. Researching keywords that not only reflect what you want to rank for but also what your potential customers are searching for is key. I always recommend investing time in this foundational element. A strong keyword strategy involves a mix of short-tail and long-tail keywords to capture a broader audience while still focusing on niche markets. This allows you to target various stages of the customer journey, from awareness to consideration and eventually to conversion.

Moreover, having high-quality, relevant content is paramount. It's not just about ranking; it's about providing value. Creating content that resonates with your audience fosters engagement and encourages sharing, which can signal to search engines that your content is worthy of high rankings. Regularly updating old content and adding fresh insights also plays a critical role in maintaining relevance in search results. Beyond content, technical SEO aspects, such as site speed, mobile-friendliness, and a clear site structure, need to be prioritized. These elements contribute to how both users and search engines perceive your site, affecting overall performance.

In an ever-evolving digital world, adaptability is a crucial element of any lasting SEO strategy. Search engine algorithms are constantly changing, and what worked a few months ago might not have the same impact today. This is why it's important to stay informed about industry trends and algorithm updates. Continuous learning and adjusting your strategy accordingly can help keep your site competitive. Regular audits of your SEO performance can help identify what is working and what isn't. By analyzing data from various metrics, you can refine your approach to target the most effective techniques.

Being flexible allows you to experiment with new tools, technologies, and methods. Content marketing, for instance, is a field that is always in flux. Keeping an eye on emerging formats, like video or interactive content, can provide you with new avenues to reach your audience. Social media integration also plays a role; adapting your SEO strategy to leverage these platforms can enhance your visibility and engagement significantly. Remember, adaptability isn't just about reacting to changes; it's also about being proactive in identifying opportunities for improvement. Testing and iterating should be part of your regular workflow to ensure your SEO tactics remain effective in a constantly changing environment.

One practical tip is to conduct quarterly reviews of your SEO strategy. This can keep you aware of emerging trends and allow you to pivot your approach based on real-time performance data. Consistency combined with adaptability is what truly sets sustainable SEO strategies apart.

5.3 Balancing Short-Term Gains with Long-Term Growth

Achieving a balance between short-term gains and long-term growth in the realm of SEO can seem challenging but is crucial for sustained success. One effective strategy is to optimize for low-competition keywords that still have decent search volume. These keywords often allow for quicker rankings and can drive immediate traffic. By focusing on these terms, webmasters can experience a quick boost while laying the groundwork for broader, competitive terms that will enhance their site's authority over time.

Another key approach is to implement on-page SEO best practices. This includes optimizing title tags, meta descriptions, and content with the right keywords. A well-structured website with a strong internal linking strategy not only helps in garnering quick traffic but strengthens the overall site architecture, aiding in long-term crawlability and indexability by search engines. Additionally, using schema markup can enhance search visibility and improve click-through rates, contributing to both immediate and sustained success.

Combining content marketing with SEO can also yield beneficial results. Creating high-quality, valuable content that answers user queries can attract quick visitors through organic search. Moreover, content that garners social shares can help boost domain authority and improve rankings over time, creating an ongoing cycle of benefits. Consistently refreshing older content to keep it relevant can further help in maintaining rankings while appealing to new search trends.

Identifying quick wins in your SEO strategy requires a nuanced approach that prioritizes sustainable practices. One way to find these quick wins is through regular content audits. By analyzing your existing content, you can identify posts that need updates, can be repurposed, or are already ranking well. Small tweaks, like improving the structure and adding recent information, can elevate lower-performing pages and ensure they provide maximum value to visitors without straying from your long-term goals.

Optimizing for local SEO can offer rapid results, especially if your business has a physical presence. By claiming your Google My Business listing, ensuring consistent NAP (Name, Address, Phone) information across all platforms, and prompting reviews from satisfied customers, you can quickly improve your local search visibility. This localized focus can yield quick returns while encouraging loyalty and repeat visits, contributing to long-term customer relationships.

Focusing on link-building campaigns that prioritize quality over quantity can also uncover quick wins. Engaging in guest blogging or partnerships with reputable sites can lead to immediate backlinks while also building a network that benefits your long-term authority. Each link established not only aids in enhancing your rankings but also helps create valuable relationships in your industry. Balancing these short-term strategies with your overarching vision will ensure that your SEO journey is fruitful in both the present and the future.

Finding the sweet spot in this balance often comes down to being proactive and analytical. Consider monitoring your analytics closely to gauge the success of both your short-term strategies and long-term initiatives. This vigilance will help you adapt, ensuring that every step taken moves you closer to your overarching goals while also providing immediate results.

5.4 Incorporating Keywords Naturally in Your Content

Incorporating keywords into your writing should feel like an organic part of your narrative rather than a clumsy addition. The key to this seamless integration lies in understanding how to embed keywords within context. Start by selecting keywords that genuinely relate to your content's core message. Instead of forcing a keyword into a sentence, ask yourself how it fits in naturally. For instance, if you're writing about digital marketing strategies, instead of stuffing SEO techniques wherever possible, weave it thoughtfully into a discussion about improving website traffic. When keywords are placed logically, they enhance your message and contribute to the reader's understanding rather than detract from it.

This approach also requires focusing on sentence structure and varying your language. Repetition can become tiresome, so use synonyms and related phrases that maintain the keyword's essence while keeping the text dynamic. Engaging storytelling combined with keyword awareness can create content that resonates with both readers and search engines. Think of your writing as a conversation; you wouldn't awkwardly cram in words just for the sake of it. Instead, let your natural voice guide you, allowing keywords to flow as part of the overall experience.

Maintaining flow while optimizing for SEO may seem challenging, but with some practical strategies, you can achieve both goals. One effective practice is to prioritize content quality above all else. High-quality content naturally attracts backlinks and engagement, which positively impacts your SEO without sacrificing readability. When your focus remains on creating valuable content for your audience, keywords will naturally find their place.

Remember, the goal is to create content that serves your audience while being discoverable through search engines. A practical tip to consider is using keyword research tools to find related terms. These can help you discover phrases that might fit your writing without disrupting its flow, giving you more options for seamless integration.

5.5 Updating and Repurposing Existing Content

Refreshing outdated content is an essential practice for maintaining a vibrant online presence. To enhance relevance, it's a good idea to start by reviewing your existing articles and checking for information that may now be inaccurate or outdated. This can involve updating statistics, statistics, or facts that have changed over time, whether due to new research, trends, or industry shifts. Consider incorporating recent insights, examples, or case studies to make your content more relatable and timely. Additionally, adjusting your writing style or format can breathe new life into older posts. For instance, if a particular article is text-heavy, breaking it down into bullet points or adding visual content such as infographics or images can engage readers better and improve usability. Updating meta tags and SEO elements is also crucial; a catchy title or a more relevant description can significantly increase click-through rates.

Identifying opportunities for content repurposing is about maximizing your return on investment. Look for high-performing articles or posts—these are gems that can be transformed into different formats. A well-researched blog post could be converted into an engaging podcast episode or a video tutorial. Similarly, you can compile several related blog posts into an eBook or create a series of infographics that highlight key points. Repurposing not only saves time and effort but also helps reach a broader audience who may prefer different content types. Leverage social media channels by sharing snippets of your refreshed content to generate interest and drive traffic back to your site. By thinking creatively about how to engage with existing content, you can efficiently expand your content library and improve your overall content strategy.

To ensure the longevity of your content, always keep a calendar for regular updates. Set a schedule to revisit your older posts every few months; this will help you maintain a fresh, relevant online repository. Remember, combining the tasks of refreshing and repurposing can significantly enhance your content's impact and visibility. Keep an eye on analytics to track which updated pieces perform best, using that data to inform future content strategies. This continual adaptation not only benefits your audience but also ultimately strengthens your digital presence.

5.6 Creating an SEO Playbook

A comprehensive SEO playbook serves as a roadmap for businesses aiming to enhance their online presence through search engines. The first essential component is keyword research. Understanding what terms your audience is searching for forms the foundation of any effective SEO strategy. This involves not just identifying keywords, but also analyzing search intent, which helps you tailor content to match what users truly want to know. Utilizing tools like Google Keyword Planner or SEMrush can provide insights into keyword volume and competition, guiding your choices.

Next, on-page optimization is crucial. This includes optimizing titles, meta descriptions, headers, and content itself to ensure that they align with your chosen keywords. Good on-page SEO enhances user experience and makes it easier for search engines to understand your content. Don't overlook the importance of URL structure either. Clean, descriptive URLs can improve click-through rates and assist in search engine crawling.

Another vital part of your playbook is off-page SEO, which involves building backlinks from reputable sources. High-quality backlinks signal to search engines that your website is trustworthy and relevant. It's important to focus on ethical link-building strategies, as engaging in black-hat techniques may lead to penalties. Engaging with industry blogs, guest posting, and participating in forums can help in earning these valuable links.

Documenting your SEO processes and strategies ensures that there's consistency in execution, which is key to achieving positive results over time. Start by creating a centralized SEO document that outlines your strategies, keyword lists, and objectives. This guide should be easily accessible to your team so that everyone is on the same page regarding goals and techniques.

In your documentation, describe each tactic clearly. For instance, outline how keyword research is conducted – what tools are used, how often it should be done, and which metrics are important. Include step-by-step guidelines for on-page optimization, specifying how to write engaging meta descriptions or structure headers effectively. This clarity helps in maintaining a uniform approach to SEO across all content creators and marketers involved.

It's also beneficial to include a calendar for regular SEO audits. Set schedules for analyzing your website's performance based on analytics data. This could involve monitoring keyword rankings, evaluating traffic patterns, and assessing link-building efforts. Regular audits ensure that you stay agile in your strategies, adapting to any algorithm changes or shifts in user behavior. To make this even smoother, consider using project management tools to assign tasks related to SEO efforts and keep track of progress, so that everyone is accountable.

An easy tip to implement is to create a "SEO FAQ" document, where team members can upload queries and solutions related to SEO challenges they encounter. This resource can continually evolve, providing a living document that enhances both knowledge and efficiency in your SEO efforts.

Chapter 6: Start With Technical SEO Fundamentals

6.1 The Significance of Site Speed

Site speed plays a crucial role in shaping user experience, which is something we can never overlook as webmasters and digital marketers. When a visitor lands on a website, their experience begins with how quickly the page loads. If it takes too long, they might leave before even seeing what you have to offer. Research shows that users expect a webpage to load in two seconds or less. If the load time stretches beyond that, frustration surfaces, often leading to increased bounce rates. This immediate response influences not only user satisfaction but also perceptions of your brand. A fast site is synonymous with professional and reliable service, while a slow site can leave a visitor wondering if they can trust you. So, it's more than just speed; it's about creating a seamless journey that keeps users engaged and exploring your content or services.

There are straightforward strategies to improve site speed, and doing so can significantly enhance your SEO rankings. Optimizing images is one of the simplest yet most effective techniques. Large image files can slow down your site considerably. By compressing images without sacrificing quality, you can ensure they load quickly while keeping your visual appeal intact. Another approach is leveraging browser caching, which allows your site to store some resources locally on the user's device. This means that when a user returns, your page can load much faster because it doesn't need to download everything from scratch. Furthermore, minimizing HTTP requests by combining files also helps streamline the loading process. All these changes contribute not just to improving speed but also to a better user experience, resulting in longer visits and higher conversion rates.

Investing time into improving your site speed is worthwhile, not just for the immediate satisfaction of your users but also for your place in search engine rankings. A faster site isn't just a nice-to-have feature; it's becoming essential for online success in an increasingly competitive digital landscape. Consider running regular audits on your site's speed using tools like Google PageSpeed Insights, which provide insights tailored to your needs. Keep in mind that by prioritizing site speed, you're not only catering to your user's expectations but also enhancing your website's potential to rank higher in search engine results. The faster you are, the better your chances are for users to stick around and engage with your content or services, which in the end, is what we all aim for.

6.2 Mobile Optimization: Why It Matters Today

The growing importance of mobile optimization in SEO strategies cannot be overstated. With more than half of all global web traffic now coming from mobile devices, it's crucial to ensure that your website delivers an outstanding experience on smartphones and tablets. Search engines like Google have shifted their focus toward mobile-first indexing, meaning they primarily consider the mobile version of your site for ranking and indexing. This shift has significant implications for how we approach SEO. If your site isn't optimized for mobile, you risk being penalized in search rankings, which can translate into decreased visibility and potential revenue loss.

To create a truly mobile-friendly experience, there are several key elements you should focus on. First, ensure that your website is responsive, meaning it automatically adjusts to fit the screen size of any device. This involves using flexible grids and layouts that provide a seamless viewing experience. Additionally, speed is critical; mobile users often expect pages to load quickly. According to studies, users are likely to abandon a site if it takes more than three seconds to load. Optimize images and utilize techniques like lazy loading to enhance performance. Furthermore, consider the user interface—buttons and links should be easily clickable, with enough spacing to prevent misclicks. Navigation should be intuitive, allowing users to find what they need without frustration. Lastly, test your site on various mobile devices and browsers to ensure a consistent and effective experience across the board.

A practical tip to keep in mind is to regularly review your site's analytics to understand how mobile users are interacting with your content. Pay attention to bounce rates and user engagement metrics. If you notice higher bounce rates on mobile, it could indicate that your site isn't meeting user expectations. Adjusting your mobile strategy based on these insights can lead to improved performance and user satisfaction.

6.3 Ensuring a Secure Site with HTTPS

Site security plays a crucial role in how users perceive your website. When visitors see that your site is secure, indicated by the HTTPS and a padlock symbol, they are more likely to trust you, especially if they need to share personal information like credit card details. This sense of security significantly affects user experience; a secure site encourages users to engage more deeply with your content and services. With the rise of online threats, users are becoming increasingly cautious. If your site doesn't have HTTPS, you risk losing potential customers to competitors who do, as they might choose to browse away rather than risk their sensitive data. Furthermore, Google has openly stated that HTTPS is a ranking factor. Websites that implement HTTPS can gain a slight edge in search engine results, which means enhanced visibility and potentially increased traffic. As SEO specialists, we need to recognize that improving site security is not just about safety—it's also about gaining that crucial trust factor and better rankings on search engines.

Transitioning your website to HTTPS is a vital step toward ensuring security and building trust. The process begins with obtaining an SSL certificate. This certificate is essential for encrypting the data exchanged between your users and your website, preventing potential interception by malicious actors. Once you have the certificate, the next step is to configure your web server to support HTTPS. This part can involve some technical know-how, but many hosting providers offer easy guides or even automatic setup options. After setting up HTTPS, update your website's internal links and resources to point to their secure versions. It's crucial not to miss any references to ensure that all pages load securely, as mixed content warnings can scar user trust. Finally, implement 301 redirects from HTTP to HTTPS. This ensures that any traffic directed to your old HTTP URLs automatically goes to the secure version, preserving your SEO rankings. This transition may feel daunting, but in today's digital landscape, it's a necessary step to create a safe space for users and promote your site's success.

As a practical tip, always keep an eye on your site's performance after the transition. Use tools like Google Search Console to monitor any crawl errors and ensure everything is functioning smoothly. This diligence will help maintain your site's integrity and boost user trust.

6.4 Setting up Google Search Console, Bing webmaster Tools, and Web Analytics

To begin with, you'll want to set up Google Search Console because it is a powerful tool for monitoring your website's presence in Google search results. Start by accessing the Search Console website and signing in with your Google account. Once logged in, you'll need to add your website as a property. This involves entering your website's URL and selecting the appropriate protocol (http or https).

After that, you'll have to verify ownership by following one of several methods: uploading an HTML file, adding a meta tag to your homepage, or using Google Analytics. Each of these methods is straightforward, just pick one that suits your setup best. Once verified, take a moment to familiarize yourself with the dashboard, which gives you insights into your website's performance, search queries, and indexing status.

Next, let's dive into Bing Webmaster Tools. Setting it up is quite similar to Google's process. Visit the Bing Webmaster Tools site and sign in with a Microsoft account. Again, you'll add your website as a property and verify your ownership, typically through an XML file, assigning a meta tag, or linking to Google Analytics. After confirmation, you can access a range of features that provide crucial data regarding your site's SEO performance, including keyword research tools, crawl reports, and the ability to submit sitemaps directly to Bing. Both of these tools are essential, as they help you understand how search engines view your site, which is the first step in optimizing it effectively.

Now that your tools are set up, it's time to leverage them for comprehensive website analysis. Using Google Search Console, you can explore the 'Performance' report, which details how many clicks your site receives, your average position in search results, and the keywords driving traffic. This data is invaluable for identifying which content resonates most with your audience and where there's potential for improvement. Similarly, Bing Webmaster Tools offers insights into how your site is performing on Bing searches. It provides keyword suggestions that could help refine your SEO strategy. Don't forget that Web Analytics, whether it's Google Analytics or another platform, can further bolster your insights by revealing user behavior on your site. Tracking metrics, such as bounce rates and average session duration, allows you to see how visitors interact with your content. Always keep an eye on these analytics to fine-tune your SEO efforts.

6.5 Schema Markup Structured Data Implementation

Schema markup is a powerful tool that helps search engines understand the context of your content. By using a specific vocabulary of tags, or microdata, you can enhance the way your page appears in search results. This can lead to rich snippets, which are visual enhancements that attract more attention and can significantly increase your click-through rates. As webmasters and SEO specialists, our job is to ensure that search engines not only crawl our pages effectively but that they also comprehend the meaning behind the data we present. For example, schema markup can identify products, reviews, events, and much more, providing search engines with specific details that help categorize and rank our content in the most relevant way.

One of the most compelling reasons to dive into schema markup is its growing importance in SEO. Search engines like Google use this structured data to generate rich snippets, making search results more informative. Rich snippets display additional information like star ratings, prices, and availability right in the search results, drawing users' eyes and encouraging clicks. When users see this extra information, they're more likely to choose your link over others. Essentially, schema markup acts as a bridge that connects your content with search engines' understanding, improving your chances of ranking higher and reaching your target audience effectively.

Implementing structured data is a straightforward process that can yield significant benefits. First, identify the content on your website that can be enhanced with schema markup. This could be articles, products, local business info, events, or recipes. Once you've determined what to mark up, you can use various tools to add the proper schema markup. Google's Structured Data Markup Helper is an excellent place to start. It allows you to select the type of data you want to markup and provides a user-friendly interface to help you create the necessary code.

After you've generated your schema code, incorporate it into your HTML. Ensure that you follow Google's guidelines for adding structured data, as improper implementation can lead to errors that prevent you from seeing the benefits. Testing your code using the Rich Results Test tool will confirm if your implementation is correct. After ensuring your markup is in order, you should also monitor the effects using Google Search Console. This tool will help you track any improvements in search visibility and provide insights on how the structured data is benefitting your website.

One practical tip to remember is to stay updated on schema changes and new developments in structured data. The world of SEO is dynamic, and search engines frequently evolve their algorithms and guidelines. Keeping an eye on announcements from Google and the Schema.org website will help you adapt your strategies and maintain a competitive edge. By making schema a regular part of your SEO maintenance, you can assure continuous improvement in your site's readability and visibility.

Chapter 7: On-Page SEO Techniques

7.1 Crafting SEO-Friendly Content, Titles, and Meta Descriptions

Creating impactful titles that attract clicks is all about blending creativity with strategy. When I craft a title, I always think about the audience I want to reach. A great title should be concise but also packed with relevant keywords that resonate with what people are searching for. Using numbers in titles can draw attention, such as "5 Essential Tips for Better SEO" since people often skim through content and are drawn to lists. Additionally, using action words can spice things up; words like "discover," "unlock," or "master" can create a sense of urgency and curiosity, compelling users to click. Don't forget to keep your target audience in mind. Tailoring your title to meet their interests or pain points can significantly increase its impact. Testing different titles using A/B testing can provide insights on what really resonates with your audience. Over time, you'll develop an intuition for creating titles that capture attention and drive traffic.

When it comes to meta descriptions, they are a crucial part of enhancing search visibility. A strong meta description should summarize your content while integrating important keywords that users might search for. Aim for around 150-160 characters to ensure that the entire description is visible in search results. A compelling call to action, such as "Learn more about..." or "Find out how..." can entice users to click. It's essential to avoid generic descriptions; instead, make sure each description is unique to the page it describes. Including a value proposition, whether it's solving a problem or offering something beneficial, can make your meta description more appealing. Additionally, Google often highlights keywords in bold within search results, so ensuring these keywords are present can catch the eye even more effectively.

Always remember that both titles and meta descriptions are your first impression to potential visitors. They need to reflect not only the content but also the value you are offering. A practical tip to keep in mind is to continually evaluate and optimize your titles and meta descriptions based on performance. Use analytics tools to track which titles get more clicks and which meta descriptions lead to higher engagement rates. Adapting and refining your approaches over time will keep your content relevant and your audience engaged.

7.2 Optimizing Header Tags for Better Structure

Proper header tag usage is fundamental in web design and content structure. It serves as a blueprint for how your content is perceived both by users and search engines. Header tags not only indicate the hierarchy of information but also enhance the readability of your websites. When headers are used correctly, they guide users through the content, breaking down complex information into digestible sections. This way, visitors can quickly scan your pages and find the information they need, making their experience more enjoyable. For search engines, optimized header tags contribute to better indexing of your content. Search algorithms prioritize well-structured content, which can lead to higher rankings in search results. Using header tags appropriately signals the main topics and subtopics of your content, allowing search engines to understand it better and place it prominently in relevant searches.

To optimize header tags effectively, start with clarity and relevance. Select a clear and concise keyword for your H1 tag that reflects the main theme of the page. This is typically your page title, so make it compelling and straightforward. H2 tags should denote key subtopics. Think of them as signposts that tell readers what is coming next. Be sure to include relevant keywords where appropriate, but do so naturally. Avoid keyword stuffing; instead, focus on creating a natural flow that enhances the reader's understanding. Additionally, using H3 tags for further breakdowns ensures your content is not only easier to read but also enriches the structure. Another technique is to keep hierarchy consistent. This means using H1 for the main title, followed by H2 for major headings and H3 for subsections. Consistency allows not only a better user experience but also helps search engines crawl through your content with ease. Lastly, never underestimate the power of a well-placed call-to-action within your headings. This can encourage reader engagement and drive them towards desired actions, making your content both functional and appealing.

One practical tip is to use online tools to evaluate your header tag structure. These can provide insights on how well your headers are optimized and suggest improvements based on SEO best practices. Regularly reviewing and refining your header tags helps maintain an organized content experience and can positively impact your website's performance in search rankings.

7.3 Importance of Alt Text for Images

Alt text, or alternative text, serves as an essential component for image search optimization. When we think about images on our websites or blogs, it's easy to overlook the text that describes them. However, search engines cannot see images the way we do; they rely heavily on alt text to understand the content and context of an image. This text not only helps visually impaired users understand what's in the image but also plays a crucial role in how well those images perform in search engine results. By incorporating relevant keywords into your alt text, you can significantly enhance your chances of appearing in image search results. This means that a thoughtfully written alt description can create additional pathways for traffic to your site, as people often search for images using specific keywords that should match your alt text.

Moreover, the growing importance of visual content means that optimizing alt text is no longer just a nice-to-have but is now a necessity. This becomes particularly vital in an era where image search is booming, thanks to platforms like Google and social media sites that prioritize visual engagement. Utilizing effective alt text helps you not only with SEO but also improves user experience, making your site more accessible and appealing to a wider audience.

Creating effective alt text descriptions involves more than just throwing in a few keywords; it requires thoughtful consideration of both context and clarity. Start by describing the image in a clear and concise manner. Aim to communicate what the image portrays in a way that a person who cannot see the image would understand. Using simple language goes a long way in making your descriptions more effective. For instance, instead of saying A stunning sunset over the city skyline, you could be more straightforward and say A sunset with orange and pink hues behind tall city buildings. This provides a clearer picture to users and search engines alike.

Another best practice is to keep your alt text under 125 characters. This limit helps ensure the description remains focused and concise. It's also critical to avoid keyword stuffing, as this could lead to penalties from search engines and diminish the user experience. Remember to make your alt text relevant to the context of the surrounding content. If the image is about a pizza restaurant, make sure the alt text reflects that rather than being vague or unrelated. Lastly, always check your images after uploading to ensure the alt text appears correctly and efficiently. A small investment of time creating thoughtful alt text can yield substantial returns in terms of traffic and accessibility.

As a practical tip, consider using tools or plugins that can generate suggestions for your alt text based on existing image metadata. This can help streamline the process and ensure you're not missing out on potential optimization opportunities.

7.4 SEO Optimize Landing Pages and Pillar Pages

Creating landing and pillar pages that truly make an impact starts with understanding the purpose of each type of page. A landing page is designed for a specific campaign or offer, while a pillar page serves as a comprehensive resource centered around a broad topic. When structuring these pages, begin with a clear and compelling headline that captures attention immediately. Use high-quality images or videos to support your message, as visual elements can greatly enhance engagement. Follow this with concise, persuasive copy that speaks directly to the needs and pain points of your audience. It's important to break up the text with subheadings and bullet points to enhance readability and ensure key information is easily digestible. For pillar pages, include internal links that connect to related content throughout your site. This not only helps with SEO but also keeps visitors on your site longer, giving them more opportunities to engage with your brand.

A high-ranking landing page isn't just about having the right keywords; it's about integrating various elements that work together in harmony. Firstly, page speed is crucial. A slow-loading page can frustrate users, leading to higher bounce rates. Make sure your images are optimized and scripts are minimized. Secondly, mobile optimization is a must. With the increasing number of users browsing on their phones, your page needs to look and function smoothly on all devices. Utilize clear call-to-action (CTA) buttons that stand out and guide visitors on what to do next, such as signing up or purchasing. Additionally, social proof, such as testimonials and reviews, can enhance credibility and encourage conversions. Make sure to track metrics and utilize A/B testing to pinpoint what elements perform best and continue refining your pages based on real user behavior.

As you develop your landing and pillar pages, consider using tools like Google Analytics or heatmaps to monitor user interactions. This data can provide invaluable insights into how visitors navigate your pages, helping you make informed adjustments that improve both user experience and SEO performance.

Chapter 8: Off-page SEO and Building Backlinks

8.1 Understanding the Importance of Backlinks

Backlinks are essential for search engine optimization (SEO) because they signal to search engines that your website is a valuable source of information. When another website links to yours, it serves as a vote of confidence. The more quality backlinks you have, the better your website's chances of ranking higher in search results. Think of each backlink as a bridge leading back to your site. This connection builds trust and authority, which positive influence search engines' algorithms. By understanding this dynamic, webmasters and digital marketers can craft strategies to attract these valuable links.

Quality links are particularly impactful when it comes to establishing your site's authority. When a reputable site links to your content, it not only drives traffic but also elevates your credibility in the eyes of search engines. A single link from a respected source, such as a well-known blog or industry publication, can do more for your site's trustworthiness than several links from less reliable sites. Search engines examine the quality of the linking site, the relevance of the content, and the anchor text used. Therefore, focusing on building relationships with authoritative sites in your niche can lead to more impactful backlinks.

To grow your backlink profile effectively, consider creating high-quality, shareable content that others will want to link to. Engaging blog posts, infographics, and industry reports can attract natural backlinks from those looking to reference valuable data. Additionally, reaching out directly to other webmasters or bloggers for collaborations can also be an effective way to build links. Always remember that in the world of backlinks, quality trumps quantity. Cultivating a few strong connections is more beneficial than having a multitude of weak ones, so prioritize your efforts accordingly to enhance your site's SEO potential.

8.2 Strategies for Earning Quality Backlinks

Effective methods to secure valuable backlinks can vary significantly depending on your niche and audience, but several strategies tend to yield strong results. One of the simplest yet most effective methods is to create high-quality, shareable content. This could be anything from in-depth articles, infographics, or videos that are informative and engaging. By producing content that genuinely offers value, you entice others to reference it and link back to your website naturally. Additionally, reaching out to relevant websites and bloggers within your niche can also open doors to obtaining backlinks. Initiating conversations where you share your insights or your content can sometimes lead to them appreciating your work and linking to it without any formal requests. This is particularly effective if you've established a rapport where they come to see you as a credible source.

Guidelines for partnerships and guest blogging opportunities can further amplify your backlink strategy. When seeking guest blogging opportunities, it's important to identify websites that not only have authority in your niche but also align with your brand values. Crafting a personalized pitch that highlights what you can offer in terms of content and value is essential. This should reflect how your guest post can benefit their audience. Equally, ensure that the content you provide is original and of high quality, as this fosters relationships for future collaborations. Building partnerships with complementary businesses can also lead to mutually beneficial backlinks. Consider co-creating resources, webinars, or even podcasts that you can promote across both audiences. This shared exposure can generate backlinks while expanding your reach.

A practical tip to remember is to constantly monitor your backlink profile. Use tools to assess which of your strategies are most effective in generating quality backlinks and adjust your approach as needed. Keeping track of your progress helps to refine your efforts and ensures that you're focusing on tactics that work best for you.

8.3 Advanced Strategies for Creating Quality Backlinks

Earning high-quality backlinks often requires thinking outside the box. One innovative approach is to leverage content collaborations. By partnering with other websites or influencers in your niche, you can create joint content pieces that add value to both parties' audiences. This could be a comprehensive guide, a webinar, or even a video series. When you collaborate, you not only tap into their audience but also encourage them to link back to your site as a trusted source. Additionally, utilizing interactive content, such as quizzes or calculators, can attract links naturally. People love sharing engaging content, and a well-designed tool can lead others to reference your site as a resource, resulting in valuable backlinks.

Another strategy involves the use of broken link building. This process entails finding broken links on high-authority websites and proposing your content as a replacement. It requires some detective work—tools like Ahrefs or SEMrush can help identify these links. Once you locate a broken link, reach out to the site owner, politely letting them know about the issue while simultaneously introducing your relevant content as a potential fix. This not only helps the site owner maintain their backlink profile but also gives you an opportunity to earn a quality link in return. People appreciate helpful suggestions, and this method also builds goodwill.

Proven tactics for enhancing your backlink profile include investing in guest blogging. By writing articles for reputable sites in your industry, you can earn valuable backlinks while showcasing your expertise. Select blogs that have a strong readership and relevance to your niche for the best impact. Craft your content to be insightful and beneficial for their audience, and include links back to your own site where appropriate. This not only boosts your authority but also helps introduce your brand to new audiences.

Another effective tactic is to engage in online communities related to your field. Participating in forums, discussion groups, and Q&A sites like Quora can be a great way to build visibility and authority. By answering questions thoughtfully and providing genuine value, you can create opportunities to link back to your website where it makes sense. Remember, the key is to be authentic and helpful, rather than overtly promotional. Over time, these interactions can lead to backlinks as other users find your site valuable.

Consider also utilizing social media strategically to amplify your existing content. Share your blog posts or articles on platforms like LinkedIn, Twitter, and Facebook, and engage with your audience. When your content reaches a wider audience, it increases the likelihood of being referenced and linked by others, including industry bloggers and influencers. Cultivating a community around your brand is crucial; as you build relationships, your site will naturally gain more backlinks.

Keep in mind that consistency is key. Regularly create high-quality content and seek out opportunities for backlinks. Also, don't overlook the power of follow-up. After implementing any of these tactics, keep track of where your links are coming from, and build upon those connections. Small, consistent efforts often yield the best results when it comes to enhancing your backlink profile.

8.4 Build Links Through Competitor Analysis

Analyzing your competitors can unveil a treasure trove of backlink opportunities that you might not have discovered otherwise. Start by identifying your main competitors—those websites that not only rank well for your target keywords but also have a strong online presence. Once you have a list, tools like Ahrefs, SEMrush, or Moz can be incredibly helpful in gathering data on their backlink profiles. These tools allow you to see where your competitors are gaining their backlinks from, which can give you insights into websites that are open to linking to content similar to yours.

As you sift through the data, look for patterns. Identify which types of content are frequently linked to; for instance, are they publishing in-depth guides, engaging infographics, or expert interviews?

Understanding what attracts links can help you tailor your content creation strategy. Additionally, observe the domains that are willing to link to your competitors. If you notice multiple competitors are receiving backlinks from the same site, it indicates that this site values such connections. It's a clear signal that reaching out to them might be a fruitful endeavor for your own link-building efforts.

Once you've gathered information on where competitors are getting their backlinks, the next step is to reverse-engineer those links. This involves not just figuring out where they link from but understanding the context in which those links appear. For instance, if a competitor is linked on a high-authority blog post, delve into that post to see how the backlink was integrated. Ask yourself what specific value or insight the content provides that warranted a link. Is it a relevant statistic, a unique perspective, or a valuable resource?

Next, consider creating similar or even better content that aligns with the topics covered in the consuming blog post. Once your content is live, reach out to the same site that linked to your competitor, making a strong case for why your content is also worthy of their audience's attention. Personalization is key here; mention the specifics of their content and explain how your piece complements it. Additionally, monitoring your competitors continuously will keep you informed of any new backlinks they acquire, allowing you to stay on top of your game. Remember, consistency and quality in your outreach efforts can make all the difference in building a robust backlink profile.

Identifying and acquiring backlinks is an ongoing process, and by regularly analyzing your competitors' strategies, you can remain competitive in content marketing. One practical tip is to set aside a few hours each month to delve into competitive analysis. This way, you'll consistently unearth new opportunities and stay ahead of the curve.

8.5 Creating Link-Worthy Content

Link-worthy content is that which naturally draws attention and interest from other websites, encouraging them to link back to it. The most compelling factor is usually its originality. When you create content that offers a fresh perspective or unique insights, it immediately stands out. Additionally, content that is well-researched and factual can build trust and credibility, prompting other webmasters to share your work. High-quality visuals, engaging storytelling, and interactive elements also enhance linkability. People are generally more inclined to share content that captivates their attention and enriches their understanding. Content that answers pressing questions or solves problems often gets shared, as it adds real value to audiences. Ensuring that your content resonates with your target audience's interests and needs is crucial in making it appealing for backlinks.

Several types of content typically attract backlinks effectively. In-depth guides and tutorials often serve as excellent resources, providing comprehensive information that others are likely to share. Listicles, especially those that feature expert opinions or valuable tips, can also gain traction due to their easy-to-scan format and engaging nature. Infographics are powerful because they amalgamate complex data into visually appealing graphics, making them easily shareable on social media and various websites. Another popular format is the case study, which provides real-life examples that can validate concepts and strategies, encouraging others to reference your findings. Surveys and original research are particularly noteworthy as they generate unique data that can drive conversation and add credibility to various discussions across the web. By diversifying your content types and focusing on providing value, you significantly increase your chances of earning those precious backlinks.

Focusing on producing high-quality, engaging content will naturally lead to better backlink opportunities. It's essential to remember that the goal is not just to gain links but to create content that people genuinely want to share. Think about what makes you excited to share something with your own network. That excitement can translate into your content creation process, making you a go-to source for valuable information in your niche.

8.6 Leverage Partnerships, Blogs and Influencer Outreach

Creating effective partnerships is an essential way to enhance your website's visibility, credibility, and search engine ranking. By teaming up with other websites that share a similar target audience, you can exchange valuable links that boost both sites in the eyes of search engines and users alike. To start forming these partnerships, it's crucial to identify relevant websites in your niche that are open to collaborations. Look for those that already have a solid online presence and are committed to quality content. Once you have a few potential partners in mind, reach out to them with a proposal that clearly outlines the benefits of collaboration, such as enhanced traffic, improved SEO, and a stronger online community. Being honest and friendly in your approach can go a long way, helping to establish a rapport that makes them more receptive to your ideas.

A successful partnership isn't just about scraping backlinks; it's about creating a win-win situation. Offer to write guest posts for each other, share each other's content on social media, or collaborate on special projects. When both parties put in effort, the relationship thrives and grows, benefitting both sites significantly. Remember, the key is to provide genuine value — whether it's insightful articles, engaging social media posts, or even joint webinars. These steps foster a sense of loyalty and commitment that will ensure your partnerships flourish over time, leading to more backlinks and organic traffic.

Influencers hold a significant sway over audiences, making them ideal allies in your quest for backlinks. When you reach out to influencers, personalization is your strongest tool. Start by genuinely engaging with their content; comment on their blogs, share their posts, and show them you appreciate their work. This approach lays a solid groundwork before you ever send an outreach email. When you do decide to reach out, craft a message that reflects your understanding of their brand and audience. Explain why your content could benefit their followers and suggest how a backlink or content sharing could serve both your interests.

It might be advantageous to propose exclusive content, like an insightful article or a joint video focused on a topic resonant with both your audiences. Offering something valuable not only increases the likelihood of a positive response, but it also elevates your credibility and rapport. Additionally, consider leveraging existing relationships. If you share mutual connections, mention them to create a warmer introduction. After establishing this connection, remain respectful and genuine in your follow-up communication. It's vital to keep the line of communication open, fostering an ongoing relationship that can lead to additional collaboration opportunities down the line. A practical tip is to always track your outreach efforts. This way, you can refine your approach and learn what works well over time, ultimately creating a network of influencers excited to engage with you and your content.

8.7 Avoiding Toxic Backlinks: What to Watch Out For

Toxic backlinks can silently undermine your website's SEO performance. One major sign of such backlinks is their source. If a link comes from a site that has little or no relevance to your niche, or worse, a site that is associated with spammy practices, it can reflect poorly on your site. Another indicator is the quality of the referring page. If a page has thin content, low traffic, or is part of link farms, it's wise to consider that link suspicious. Moreover, evaluate the anchor text used in these backlinks. When you see over-optimized anchor text or phrases that appear unnatural, it's a red flag. Also, monitoring the overall health of your backlink profile can help. If you notice many links suddenly appearing, particularly from dubious sources, it could mean your site is being targeted. Utilizing tools that analyze your link profile can provide insights into potential toxins lurking in your backlink structure.

Once you've identified toxic backlinks, it's crucial to act on them to protect your SEO. The first step is to reach out to the webmasters of the sites hosting these harmful links and request removal. While this can be effective, know that it's not always successful. That's where the disavow tool comes into play. Google provides a disavow tool that allows you to tell them to ignore certain backlinks. Creating a disavow file is straightforward: compile a list of the toxic links you've identified and submit it through Google Search Console. However, use this tool with caution; disavowing too many links might unintentionally affect your site's credibility. It's also essential to regularly audit your backlinks moving forward. Use reputable SEO tools for ongoing analysis—this way, you can spot potential issues early before they escalate. Remember, maintaining a clean backlink profile not only safeguards your SEO but also enhances your site's authority in the long run.

As a practical tip, make it a habit to regularly review your backlinks. A quarterly audit of your profile can help you stay a step ahead, allowing you to address potential issues before they impact your rankings.

8.8 Use only White Hat Techniques

Shady Techniques and Why Robots are Bad For Internet
Using white hat strategies is essential for building a sustainable SEO approach that can stand the test of time. These tactics focus on creating quality content, enhancing user experience, and adhering to search engine guidelines. By concentrating on these principles, we foster not just trust with our audience but also with the search engines. This creates a foundation where our website can grow organically, without the looming threat of penalties. White hat techniques, such as optimizing content for relevant keywords, improving site speed, and ensuring mobile-friendliness, enhance our authority and improve our rankings over time. You'll find that when you put effort into genuine, user-focused strategies, the benefits compound over time and attract visitors in a meaningful way.

In contrast, many webmasters might be tempted to employ shortcuts or 'quick fixes' which can lead to immediate gains. However, while black hat tactics like keyword stuffing or cloaking might yield some short-lived success, they ultimately risk long-term damage to our online presence. Search engines are getting smarter every day, and they can penalize websites that don't play by the rules. Hence, it is wiser to commit to a path of integrity and reliability, nurturing our online reputation rather than gambling it with dubious strategies. Think of it as planting a seed and patiently waiting for it to grow, rather than forcing it to sprout with harsh methods which could harm the plant.

Black hat tactics can be incredibly risky for any website. Initially, they might seem appealing due to the quick results they promise. However, the repercussions can be severe. Many webmasters have faced penalties that lead to significant drops in their search rankings or outright removal from search engine listings. This fallout isn't just theoretical; I've seen it happen time and time again where friends and colleagues lose months or years of hard work simply because they chose to chase immediate gratification over sustainable growth. It's heartbreaking to watch someone become disheartened with their website when simple, ethical strategies could have kept them safe from harm.

Moreover, relying on these shady techniques can poison the relationship we have with our audience. When users land on a site that's manipulated to deceive them, they leave feeling frustrated and misled. This not only affects site traffic but also damages our brand's reputation. Trust is incredibly hard to rebuild once it's lost, and in the digital age, it can lead to drastic consequences for a business. By employing transparent, ethical practices, we cultivate a loyal audience that appreciates our integrity and will return for value, thus ensuring our long-term success and stability in the digital landscape.

A practical tip to enhance your SEO strategy is to regularly check for updates on search engine guidelines. Staying informed about algorithm changes can help you adapt your tactics to align with best practices and avoid algorithmic penalties.

Chapter 9: Local SEO Techniques

9.1 The Importance of Local Search for Small Businesses

Local search engine optimization, or local SEO, is a critical element for small businesses trying to carve out their space in the digital landscape. Unlike larger corporations with extensive marketing budgets, small enterprises often rely on their local communities for growth. This is where local SEO shines. By optimizing web pages to target specific local search phrases, businesses can ensure they appear in search results when potential customers are looking for services in their area. This not only increases visibility but builds trust, as local consumers often prefer to deal with businesses they recognize or can easily find in their vicinity.

Consider that most consumers today conduct searches on their mobile devices while on the go. They're searching for nearby services, restaurants, or shops, and they expect quick results. If your business is optimized for local search, you may appear at the top of these search results, attracting customers who are ready to engage. Additionally, local SEO encompasses creating a Google My Business profile, gathering positive reviews, and ensuring that your business information is consistent across online directories. These components work together to enhance your credibility and relevance in your community, often leading to increased website traffic and foot traffic to your business.

Implementing an effective local search strategy can dramatically expand your customer reach. Imagine someone searching for a coffee shop while they are strolling through your neighborhood. If your coffee shop has optimized its website with local keywords, claimed its Google My Business listing, and received positive reviews, there's a much higher chance that the searcher will discover your establishment. This immediacy can turn a casual browser into a loyal customer. Local search not only brings in new customers but also allows businesses to cultivate relationships and maintain repeat patronage.

Moreover, the beauty of local search lies in its nurturing potential. When your business appears in local search results, especially on map services, you're positioned not just as another option, but as an accessible choice for your targeted demographic. This accessibility fosters community loyalty, which can lead to word-of-mouth referrals that are invaluable to small businesses. Providing excellent service that encourages customers to leave positive reviews can enhance this pattern, creating a cycle of growth and engagement. Remember, optimizing for local search can turn casual searches into meaningful connections, ultimately expanding your customer base far beyond what you might have originally thought possible.

Investing time and effort into your local SEO strategy can create significant returns. A practical tip is to regularly update your Google My Business listing with new photos, posts, and business hours. Active engagement on this platform communicates to potential customers that your business is vibrant and open for business, making it more likely they'll choose you over the competition.

9.2 Creating and Optimizing Your Google My Business Listing

Creating a Google My Business profile is both a straightforward and essential step for any business looking to establish local visibility. Start by visiting the Google My Business website and clicking on the "Manage now" button. You'll then be prompted to enter your business name. If it exists in Google's database, it may auto-suggest it, which can save time. If your business isn't listed, you can easily create a new entry. After entering your business name, the next step is to fill in the essential details like the address, service area, and phone number. Make sure that your address is accurate and consistent with what's on your website and social media pages, as this consistency helps improve your overall SEO. When adding your business category, choose the most relevant one, as this will help Google understand your business better and display it in appropriate search results.

One crucial part of the setup process is verifying your business. Google typically does this via a postcard sent to your business address, which includes a verification code. Enter this code to prove that you're the rightful owner of the business. Once verified, focus on optimizing your listing by adding high-quality images. Photos of your products, services, or even your storefront can significantly enhance your profile. Regular updates to your listing are important as well; encourage customer reviews, respond promptly to questions, and update your hours during holidays or special events. All these elements combined help create a robust Google My Business profile that not only attracts more clicks but also gives potential customers a taste of what they can expect from your business.

The benefits of having a well-optimized Google My Business listing cannot be overstated. An optimized listing improves your chances of appearing in local search results, especially in the coveted local pack, where Google showcases top businesses related to a search query. Increased visibility translates into higher foot traffic and, ultimately, more sales. Beyond just visibility, a good listing boosts your credibility. Customers often look for reviews and ratings before making a decision, so positive experiences shared by others can work in your favor. An optimized Google My Business profile can also help improve your website ranking because Google takes into account the quality of the information provided. By maintaining a fully filled-out profile with accurate and engaging content, you increase your chances of being shown prominently in searches related to your services. Additionally, consider using Google Posts to share updates, promotions, or events, further enhancing customer engagement. Remember, the key to standing out lies in authenticity and consistency, so make sure your profile reflects your brand's personality while remaining easy to navigate.

To maximize your listings' effectiveness, it's a good idea to regularly check your insights. Google provides valuable data on how consumers find your listing, how they interact with it, and what actions they take. This information can guide your ongoing optimization efforts, allowing you to adapt your strategy to what actually works. Keep experimenting with different approaches to see how they impact your visibility and customer engagement.

9.3 Gathering and Managing Customer Reviews

Customer reviews play a pivotal role in shaping a business's online presence, especially in the realm of local SEO. They not only provide social proof but also enhance a company's visibility in search results. When potential customers see positive reviews, they are more likely to trust your business and consider it credible. Search engines like Google recognize this and often factor in the quantity and quality of reviews when determining local search rankings. High ratings can lead to rich snippets in search results, which showcase star ratings and can greatly increase click-through rates. The geographical relevance is also crucial; positive local reviews signal to search engines that your business is a trusted option within the community. This means that for webmasters and SEO specialists, actively gathering and managing customer reviews is essential not only for customer engagement but also for improving local search engine performance.

Encouraging and managing reviews effectively requires thoughtful strategies that prioritize customer experience. One effective approach is to simplify the review process. When customers know that leaving a review is quick and easy, they are far more likely to follow through. Utilizing follow-up emails or SMS messages post-purchase can serve as reminders. Importantly, it's vital to ask for feedback at optimal moments; timing is everything. If a customer has just had an excellent experience, they are more inclined to share their thoughts. Offering incentives can also motivate customers, but ensure that it's in compliance with the review platform's guidelines. However, it's essential to foster genuine engagement rather than simply chasing numbers. When reviewing, always respond to customer feedback, whether it's positive or negative. This shows that you value their opinions and are committed to improving their experience. Remember that negative reviews can provide an opportunity to demonstrate your customer service and willingness to address issues while showcasing that you care about your clientele.

9.4 Build Local Citations and Listings

Local citations are mentions of your business's name, address, and phone number (often referred to as NAP) across various online platforms. These citations help establish your business's presence within a specific area and are critical for local SEO, as they signal to search engines that your business is legitimate and relevant to local users. For instance, if someone searches for best pizza in Chicago, search engines use local citations to determine which businesses to display. Consistent and accurate citations can improve your rankings in local search results, enhance your visibility to potential customers, and lead to increased foot traffic to your physical business location.

When people see your business listed on trusted sites, it boosts your credibility and encourages them to choose your services over competitors who may lack reliable citations.

Maintaining consistency across various business listings is essential for the credibility and ranking of your local business. Start by making a comprehensive list of all platforms where your business is listed, including directories, social media, and review sites. It's vital that your NAP details are consistent across all these platforms; even small discrepancies can confuse users and search engines. Double-check spellings, abbreviations, and formats of your business name and address. If you have multiple locations, ensure each is clearly defined in its respective listing. Using a trusted service or software can help you manage and verify your citations systematically, ensuring each entry matches perfectly. Keeping your information up to date is also crucial; for example, if you change your phone number or move to a new location, update your details immediately everywhere you're listed to avoid disrupting your visibility. Consistent citations not only improve your local SEO but also foster trust with your potential customers, helping them find and connect with your business easily.

Regular audits can help you identify and correct any inconsistencies in your listings. Tools are available that can monitor and alert you to discrepancies, making the process much more manageable. Taking proactive steps to build and maintain clean, consistent citations will pay off significantly in improving your local search presence.

9.5 Use Local Keywords. Create Location-Specific Landing Pages

Identifying local keywords that resonate with your audience is essential for tailoring your online presence. Start by thinking like your potential customers. What terms would they use when searching for services you provide? Use tools like Google Keyword Planner or SEMrush to find keywords that are popular in your specific geographical area. Long-tail keywords that include your location often yield better results because they match what locals are actually searching for. For instance, instead of just targeting pizza, consider phrases like best pizza in [city name] or pizza delivery in [neighborhood name]. By focusing on these localized terms, you create a stronger connection with your community and improve your chances of capturing local traffic.

Best practices for creating location-specific landing pages involve a few key strategies. First, make sure each landing page targets a specific location and features relevant content about that area. Include not just the local keywords, but also mentions of local landmarks, events, or community highlights. This not only assists with SEO but also shows that you're engaged with the local community. It's also wise to keep your messaging consistent across all pages, ensuring that your branding and tone reflect your business identity while appealing to the local culture. Include clear calls to action and easy navigation to guide visitors towards booking your services. Optimizing for mobile is crucial, as many users will search for services on-the-go, particularly when they're in your vicinity.

Another tip to consider is optimizing your landing pages with local data. Adding structured data markup can help search engines understand your content better and may improve your visibility in local searches. Including a Google Maps widget can reinforce your location's significance, while social proof like customer reviews can enhance credibility. Don't forget to maintain a blog with localized content to keep your website fresh and relevant. Regularly updated content shows search engines and your visitors that your business is active and in tune with the local area. This approach can lead to increased engagement and, ultimately, higher conversion rates.

9.6 Engage in Link-Building with Local Websites

and Focus on Localized Content Marketing
Establishing local partnerships for backlink opportunities is crucial for anyone looking to enhance their online visibility. Most businesses thrive in their communities, and tapping into this local ecosystem can significantly elevate your website's authority. Start by identifying businesses, organizations, or even blogs in your area that complement your offerings. For instance, if you run a local bakery, partnering with a nearby coffee shop creates a natural synergy. You could contribute a guest post on their blog about the

perfect pastries to pair with specific coffee types, and in exchange, they could link back to your website. This kind of collaboration not only gives you valuable backlinks but also introduces your brand to a wider local audience. Attend local business meetups, sponsor community events, or even engage with local online forums to establish these connections. Always remember, genuine relationships often lead to the best partnership opportunities, and it's worth putting in the effort to build trust and credibility within your community.

The importance of localized content marketing strategies cannot be overstated when it comes to boosting visibility. Search engines like Google prioritize local relevance, making it vital for webmasters and digital marketers to tailor their content specifically for their target audience's geographic area. By creating blog posts, articles, and social media content that resonates with local culture, events, and interests, you're not just attracting visitors; you're attracting the right visitors. Share stories about local sponsorships, highlight client testimonials from local customers, or provide guides to local attractions that relate to your services. This localization helps search engines understand that your business is a relevant resource within the community, which can positively impact your local search rankings. Additionally, consider utilizing local keywords effectively, as it ensures your content remains search-friendly while directly appealing to your audience's immediate needs.

Combining these local partnerships with tailored content marketing forms a powerful strategy for enhancing both your SEO and community engagement. A practical tip is to regularly evaluate the performance of your local content versus broader content. Are your community-focused blog posts drawing more traffic? Is there an uptick in local inquiries after collaborating with another local business? Not only does this data help refine your approach, but it also ensures that your efforts in link-building and content marketing are leading to tangible results. Keep experimenting, remain open to adjustments, and allow your local relationships to flourish as you create a unique digital footprint tailored to your community.

9.7 Schema Markup for Local SEO

Schema markup plays a crucial role in local SEO by enhancing how search engines understand the information on your website. It is a form of structured data that helps to provide context to your content. When you use schema markup effectively, search engines are better positioned to index your website accurately and display relevant information. This is particularly important for local businesses seeking to improve their visibility in search results. By implementing schema markup, you can assist search engines in identifying your business name, address, phone number, operating hours, and other key details. This extra clarity can lead to rich snippets in search results, helping to draw more attention to your listings and improving click-through rates.

Implementing local schema markup is more straightforward than it may appear. Start by identifying the specific types of schema that apply to your business, like the LocalBusiness schema, which includes vital attributes such as location, contact information, and services offered. You can easily add schema markup to your website through various methods. For many platforms, plugins are available that can automatically generate the correct markup for you. If you prefer a hands-on approach, use a JSON-LD format, which is recommended by Google for structured data. Adding schema markup to your website's code can aid in creating an enhanced listing in local search results, giving potential customers immediate access to essential details about your business.

One practical tip is to use Google's Structured Data Testing Tool to validate your schema markup implementation. This tool can help you check if your markup is implemented correctly and highlight any errors that may need fixing. By ensuring your schema is accurate, you increase the chances of your site appearing prominently in local searches, thereby attracting more traffic and potential customers. Stay proactive about updating your schema as your business information changes, such as new operating hours or updated service offerings, to ensure you remain relevant in search results.

Chapter 10: Integrating SEO with Other Marketing Strategies

10.1 The Relationship Between SEO and Content Marketing

Content marketing and SEO go hand in hand, creating a powerful duo that can elevate your online presence. Content marketing focuses on creating valuable and relevant content to attract and engage your target audience, while SEO is all about optimizing that content so it can be easily found by search engines. When you produce high-quality content that satisfies the needs of your audience, you not only build authority but also improve your site's chance of ranking higher in search results. This mutually beneficial relationship means that every blog post, video, or infographic you create can serve as a landing point for potential visitors, driving traffic and engagement.

Moreover, great content naturally attracts backlinks, which are crucial for SEO. When other websites link to your content, it signals to search engines that your content is valuable and trustworthy. This, in turn, boosts your rankings. Thus, by investing time in crafting comprehensive and engaging pieces of content, you set yourself up for long-term SEO success. It's like giving a gift that keeps on giving—content that continues to perform well long after it's published, helping both your audience and search engine crawlers to find value in what you have to say.

To effectively integrate content marketing with SEO, you want to start with thorough keyword research. Understanding what your audience is searching for allows you to create content that answers their questions and meets their needs. Use these keywords strategically in your titles, headings, and throughout the body of your content, ensuring they're woven seamlessly into the narrative. However, avoid keyword stuffing; the focus should remain on providing value to your readers first and foremost.

Another best practice is to incorporate various types of content. Mix text with images, videos, and even interactive elements to keep your audience engaged. Not only does this improve the user experience, but it also opens the door for different SEO opportunities. For instance, optimizing video content with proper tags and descriptions can help it surface in search results. Additionally, making sure your content is mobile-friendly is essential, as search engines prioritize websites that offer a good experience across all devices.

Regularly updating your content can also have a significant impact. Search engines appreciate fresh content, so revisiting older articles to update information, add new insights, or optimize for better keywords can bring new life to your site. Engaging with your audience through comments and social media can provide insights into what resonates with them, guiding your future content strategy. By continuously evaluating both your SEO performance and the effectiveness of your content, you can ensure that both strategies work synergistically, leading to remarkable growth and visibility online.

Invest your time in understanding how your audience consumes content and the challenges they face. This knowledge can guide your content creation and optimization efforts, ensuring you not only meet but exceed their expectations.

10.2 Importance of Content Marketing as Advanced SEO Strategy

Content marketing is at the core of SEO success because it serves multiple purposes. First, it provides value to your audience, creating engagement and leading to organic traffic. When your content resonates with readers, they are more likely to share it, which generates backlinks and signals to search engines that your site is worth visiting. The more high-quality content you produce, the more opportunities you have to rank for relevant keywords. This is crucial, as search engines prioritize content that answers users' queries effectively. Recent studies show that businesses investing in content marketing see higher conversion rates and improved search ranking, demonstrating its undeniable link to SEO performance.

Leveraging content marketing also involves building authority in your niche. By consistently producing quality content, you establish yourself as an expert. This expertise not only attracts users but also encourages other sites within your industry to link to you, further enhancing your SEO. Engaging blog posts, detailed guides, or insightful infographics provide the kind of valuable information that others will reference and share. This authority can transform your website from just another entry in the vast expanse of the internet into a trusted source of information. Additionally, engaging with your audience through comments or social media helps foster relationships, which can lead to long-term loyalty and increased traffic. The more you actively engage and contribute, the more you'll strengthen your reputation as a credible source within your industry.

One practical tip is to focus on creating pillar content that serves as a comprehensive resource for a specific topic. By developing in-depth guides or articles and linking related content back to it, you can naturally enhance your SEO and authority simultaneously. This strategy not only improves user experience but also allows search engines to better understand your site's structure and the relevance of your content.

10.3 Utilizing Social Media for SEO Gains, Linkedin and Others

Social media channels can significantly enhance your SEO visibility when used strategically. Each tweet, post, and share can lead potential visitors back to your website, improving your overall search rankings. Begin by ensuring that your social profiles are optimized with relevant keywords related to your business. When you create content, whether it's a blog post or an infographic, share it across all your social media platforms immediately. Each share acts like a vote of confidence, signaling to search engines that your content is worth noticing.

Additionally, don't underestimate the power of engaging multimedia content. Videos and images tend to garner more likes, shares, and comments, which can amplify your SEO efforts. Platforms like LinkedIn are particularly beneficial for professionals and businesses looking to establish authority in their field. Posting informative articles, updates, and industry insights can help attract a targeted audience and drive traffic back to your site. The key is to integrate your social media presence with your existing SEO strategy, fostering a symbiotic relationship where each channel supports the other.

Best practices for engaging users on social platforms revolve around consistent interaction and authentic communication. Responding to comments and messages promptly can create a community around your brand. It's imperative to ask questions and encourage discussions that matter to your audience. Use polls or surveys to spark interest, and share user-generated content to foster a sense of belonging among your followers. Remember, the more engaged your audience feels, the more likely they are to share your content. This not only helps in building trust but also in extending your reach organically, which is a crucial aspect for both social media and SEO efficacy. Always think about how you can provide value to your followers while subtly promoting your brand and encouraging site visits.

Leverage analytics tools provided by these social platforms to refine your approach. Pay attention to which types of posts generate the most engagement, then double down on those strategies. Continuous learning and adaptation are vital in both social media and SEO landscapes. Lastly, consider collaborating with influencers or industry experts on your social channels to enhance your credibility and reach.

10.4 Email Marketing's Role in Driving Traffic

Email marketing can significantly bolster your SEO efforts. When you send out emails, you're not just communicating with your subscribers; you're also driving traffic back to your website. This increased traffic can lead to more page views and a lower bounce rate, two factors that search engines consider when determining your site's ranking. Moreover, when you provide valuable content through your emails, you encourage your recipients to engage with your website in meaningful ways, such as sharing that content or linking back to it from their own platforms.

One of the most effective ways email marketing supports your SEO is through content distribution. If you're creating quality blog posts, articles, or resources, sharing these via email not only keeps your audience informed but also brings them back to your site. Each time a recipient clicks a link in your email, it signals to search engines that your content is engaging and relevant, which can positively affect your rankings. Additionally, when you encourage readers to share your content, you amplify its reach and potential backlinks, further enhancing your SEO profile.

Integrating email campaigns into your overall SEO strategy requires a thoughtful approach. Start by segmenting your email lists based on user behavior and preferences, which allows you to tailor your messages more effectively. When your emails provide content that resonates with specific segments of your audience, the likelihood of engagement increases, which drives more traffic to your site and improves your SEO.

Another effective strategy is to utilize analytics. By analyzing how your emails influence website traffic and engagement, you can refine your campaigns to be more effective. Track the performance of links in your emails using UTM parameters. This data reveals which campaigns are driving the most traffic and engagement, allowing you to optimize future efforts based on solid insights.

Finally, consider sending out regular newsletters that highlight popular posts, new content, or industry updates. This not only keeps your audience engaged but also encourages repeat visits to your website. Remember, every email is an opportunity to drive traffic, and making the most of those opportunities can greatly enhance your SEO efforts.

Chapter 11: SEO Tools and Resources

11.1 The Must-Have SEO Tools in Your Arsenal

(Google Search Console, Web Analytics, AI Assistant, Pseudo Metrics such as MOZ, and Others)

Effective SEO management is largely about having the right tools at your disposal. From understanding how users find your website to analyzing the effectiveness of your content, essential tools like Google Search Console and various web analytics platforms are invaluable. These tools help us monitor traffic, fix issues, and optimize our sites to improve rankings. Google Search Console, for instance, allows us to see search impressions, clicks, and errors, while web analytics gives insights into user behavior. By leveraging these tools, we can drive our SEO efforts, making data-backed decisions that enhance our strategies over time.

Choosing the right tools can significantly influence your SEO success. It's important to align them with your specific goals, whether you're aiming for increased traffic, better engagement, or enhanced conversion rates. Take the time to evaluate what aspects of your SEO you need help with. For smaller websites, basic tools might suffice, while more extensive operations may require advanced metrics and analytics capabilities. Consider tools like MOZ for tracking pseudo metrics, as they provide additional insights into domain authority and link building. As the SEO landscape constantly evolves, incorporating AI-based assistants can streamline research and content creation, serving as a valuable resource in today's dynamic environment.

One practical tip is to regularly review the tools in your SEO arsenal. Technology evolves, and what worked a year ago may not be the best option today. Stay abreast of emerging tools and updates to existing ones. Periodically adjusting your toolkit can lead to improved performance and more effective SEO strategies, ensuring that you are always in line with the best practices and current standards in the industry.

11.2 Using Analytics to Inform Your Strategy

Data analytics plays a crucial role in shaping and improving your SEO strategies. When I first dove into the world of digital marketing, I quickly realized that intuition alone doesn't cut it. Relying on gut feelings or outdated assumptions can lead us down the wrong path. Instead, using data analytics allows us to understand what is actually happening with our audience and how they interact with our content. By examining metrics like organic traffic, bounce rates, and conversion rates, we can gain insights into not only what is working but also what isn't. This gives us a clearer picture of our users' behavior, preferences, and pain points.

With the wealth of information available today, data analytics serves as a lighthouse guiding us through the often murky waters of SEO. Every click, search term, and visitor action can be tracked and analyzed. For instance, tools like Google Analytics provide invaluable data about user engagement across various pages on your site. By identifying the high-performing keywords and the content that resonates best with your audience, you can refine your SEO approach and focus on strategies that yield the highest returns. This ability to pivot based on solid data rather than assumptions ensures that your strategies are aligned with real customer needs.

Leveraging analytics insights means making informed decisions that can dramatically enhance your online presence. I often utilize tools that help me visualize this data, making it easier to spot trends and anomalies. For example, if a particular webpage sees a sudden spike in traffic, I delve deeper to understand what might have caused it. Was it a blog post that just went viral, or perhaps it was featured in an influential publication? Understanding these factors can help replicate that success in the future.

Additionally, analytics can highlight underperforming pages that might need a fresh perspective or optimization. If certain keywords aren't bringing traffic as expected, it might be time for a content overhaul or to rethink the keyword strategy altogether. Adjustments can also extend to technical SEO elements if data shows that mobile users have a higher bounce rate on a specific page. With this knowledge, we can implement targeted changes to improve user experience. All this adds up to a cycle of continuous improvement, where each insight informs the next strategy.

It's not just about reacting to what analytics tells us; we can also proactively use it to enhance our target audience's experience. By segmenting users based on their behavior patterns or demographics, we can tailor our approach to meet diverse user needs. This ensures that our website remains a valuable resource for all visitors, leading to better engagement and higher conversion rates. As you analyze your data, always keep an eye on actionable insights, focusing on how you can tweak your strategies to stay ahead of the curve.

11.3 Coursera and other Resources for Continuous Learning and Improvement

Online learning platforms have transformed the way we acquire new skills, especially in the ever-evolving world of SEO. With countless resources at our fingertips, webmasters, digital marketers, and SEO specialists can easily stay updated with the latest trends and techniques. Coursera, for example, offers courses from top universities and companies that cover everything from the fundamentals of SEO to advanced strategies that can give us a competitive edge. The flexibility of these online courses means we can learn at our own pace, making it easier to balance our professional development with our daily responsibilities.

When looking for courses to enhance SEO skills, I highly recommend checking out specific offerings on platforms like Coursera. Courses such as Search Engine Optimization (SEO) by the University of California, Davis, provide a comprehensive overview of SEO concepts, including keyword research, link building, and analytics. Additionally, consider exploring their specialization series, which dives deeper into each aspect of SEO. But don't stop there—expand your search to other resources. Websites like Moz, HubSpot Academy, and SEMrush Academy offer free courses and materials that can further refine your skills and understanding of the industry's best practices. By engaging with various sources, we can cultivate a more rounded perspective on SEO and how to apply it effectively in our projects.

One practical tip for maximizing the value of these courses is to create a dedicated learning schedule. By designating specific times each week to focus solely on online learning, you create a habit that fosters consistent growth. Implement what you learn in real-time by applying new techniques to your current projects. Another helpful strategy is to connect with peers in the industry; discussing course content or sharing insights can deepen your understanding while building a support network. Embracing continuous learning not only enhances our skills but also keeps our strategies fresh and relevant to the fast-paced world of digital marketing.

Chapter 12: Understanding Metrics and Pseudo Metrics in SEO

12.1 Understanding Google Metrics and the Limitations of Pseudo Metrics Like Moz

Google's PageRank, once the cornerstone of its ranking algorithm, was officially removed from public view in **April 2016**, when Google discontinued the public Toolbar PageRank metric. While PageRank still exists internally as part of Google's ranking system, it is no longer accessible to SEOs or website owners. The original system assigned numerical values to web pages based on their link structure, influencing rankings significantly. However, due to widespread manipulation through link buying and spammy tactics, Google gradually phased out public access to PageRank, replacing it with more complex, undisclosed ranking factors that evaluate content quality, relevance, and user experience rather than just link equity.

When evaluating SEO, it's crucial to understand the key metrics that are vital for assessing a website's health and performance. Google metrics, such as PageRank, organic traffic levels, and bounce rates, provide a detailed view of your site's effectiveness in search engines. For example, PageRank measures the importance of your site based on the quantity and quality of backlinks, while organic traffic indicates the number of visitors arriving through unpaid search results. The bounce rate shows how many visitors leave a page without interaction. Together, these metrics offer valuable insights into your site's visibility and user engagement, aiding informed decision-making for enhancing your SEO strategy.

Moz's Domain Authority (DA) and similar metrics like Ahrefs' Domain Rating (DR) and Semrush's Authority Score are **pseudo-metrics** because they have no direct connection to Google's ranking algorithm. These scores are generated using proprietary methods based on factors like backlink profiles, but they do not incorporate real Google ranking signals, search intent analysis, or user behavior data. Since Google does not share its ranking factors with third-party tools, these metrics are simply approximations based on limited data from independent crawlers, which do not match Google's vast index. As a result, DA, DR, and similar scores can be highly inaccurate, often overestimating or underestimating a site's actual ability to rank, making them unreliable for serious SEO decision-making.

However, caution is warranted when interpreting pseudo metrics, which can distort perceptions of SEO performance. Tools like Moz, Ahrefs', SEMrush, and others offer various metrics that, while beneficial, may not accurately reflect true search engine ranking potential. For instance, Moz's Domain Authority provides a score based on link metrics, but this score often doesn't correlate with actual Google rankings. Such discrepancies can mislead SEO specialists into prioritizing score improvements rather than implementing effective strategies to boost real organic traffic. Pseudo metrics can shape perceptions of success, sometimes driving misguided strategies that focus on improving scores instead of addressing the fundamental factors affecting search performance.

Recognizing the difference between essential metrics and pseudo metrics is vital for webmasters and digital marketers alike. Regularly reviewing data from Google Analytics and Search Console can yield more actionable insights compared to relying solely on third-party tools. Balancing your monitoring efforts is beneficial, using pseudo metrics as supplementary aid rather than the primary focus. By concentrating on core metrics that truly impact performance, you can develop a more effective SEO strategy that enhances rankings while building a genuine connection with your audience.

12.2 Analyzing Traffic Sources and User Behavior

Traffic sources are the various paths through which visitors arrive at your website. Understanding these sources is crucial for any webmaster or digital marketer, as they help you identify where your audience comes from, how they interact with your content, and what channels are most effective in driving engagement. Common traffic sources include organic search, paid search, social media, direct visits, and referral links from other websites. Each of these sources has its own significance. For instance, organic search traffic indicates that your SEO efforts are paying off, while social media traffic can show how well your content resonates with users on those platforms. By analyzing these sources, you gain valuable insights into your marketing strategies, allowing you to allocate resources more effectively and refine your approach based on what works best.

To analyze user behavior, various methods can be employed to gather and interpret data that informs your strategies. Tools like Google Analytics provide comprehensive metrics on how users navigate your site. You can track page views, time spent on pages, and bounce rates, all of which indicate how engaging your content is. Heatmaps are another effective tool, as they visually represent where users click and how they scroll on your site. By examining these patterns, you can identify which areas of your site are most appealing or if there are any roadblocks that might deter users. Surveys and feedback forms also play a significant role in understanding user motivations and preferences. Engaging directly with your audience allows you to gather qualitative data that can complement your quantitative findings. This two-pronged approach not only informs your current strategies but also helps in shaping future content and marketing efforts.

It's important to remember that analyzing traffic sources and user behavior is not a one-time task but an ongoing process. Regularly revisiting your data allows you to adapt to changing trends and refine your tactics as needed. A practical tip is to set up regular reporting intervals—monthly, for example—where you assess not just traffic numbers but also the behavior patterns of users. This ensures that you're always looking at the right metrics in relation to your goals, and it helps you stay ahead in a rapidly changing digital landscape.

12.3 Interpreting Rankings and Visibility Metrics

Understanding and assessing ranking metrics effectively requires more than just looking at numbers. It's essential to dive into what these rankings signify. A high ranking on search engine results pages (SERPs) can be thrilling, but we need to ask ourselves, Why did we achieve this ranking? Factors like keyword relevance, content quality, and user experience all play crucial roles. It's also important to consider the context of these rankings. Are we ranking for competitive keywords or long-tail keywords? Are we monitoring trends over time to see if our rankings are stable or fluctuating? Consistently tracking rankings alongside traffic data helps create a comprehensive picture. This approach not only helps us appreciate our current standing but also guides our strategies moving forward.

Visibility metrics are crucial benchmarks in determining SEO success. They provide insights into how often your website appears in search results, which influences how many visitors you might attract. Higher visibility means more potential clicks, and this is where understanding metrics like impressions, click-through rates (CTR), and average positions becomes vital. When your site has high visibility, it indicates healthy organic traffic patterns and reflects the effectiveness of your SEO efforts. One can't underestimate the impact of visibility on brand awareness; when users see your website frequently in search results, it builds trust. To maximize visibility, we need to analyze the data continuously, adjusting our tactics based on what's working and what's not.

If there's one thing to take away from assessing rankings and visibility metrics, it's the importance of consistent analysis. Regularly revisiting your strategies based on data will not only keep your site competitive but will also foster a growth mindset. By focusing on both rankings and visibility, you'll set yourself up for long-term success in the ever-evolving digital landscape.

12.4 Conversion Tracking: From Click to Customer

Tracking conversions and user engagement is essential for understanding how users interact with your website. One effective strategy involves implementing comprehensive analytics tools like Google Analytics or Tag Manager. These platforms allow you to set specific goals, such as tracking form submissions, product purchases, or newsletter sign-ups. By monitoring these actions, you can gain valuable insights into where users drop off in the conversion process. Another method is to utilize UTM parameters in your URLs to track specific campaigns. This information helps you analyze which marketing efforts drive the most valuable traffic, enabling you to refine your strategies accordingly. Additionally, heatmaps can be instrumental in understanding user behavior on your site, showing where visitors click most often and how far they scroll down a page. By combining these different approaches, you create a clearer picture of user engagement and can optimize your website for better conversion rates.

The importance of conversion tracking in evaluating SEO success cannot be overstated. While high traffic is a positive indicator, it doesn't necessarily mean those visitors are engaging with your content or converting into customers. By tracking conversions, you can assess the effectiveness of your organic search efforts. For instance, if you notice that a particular landing page attracts lots of clicks but few conversions, this could signal that the content isn't resonating with users or that there are barriers in the conversion process. This data allows you to fine-tune your SEO strategy, focusing on keywords that not only generate traffic but also lead to significant user interactions. Understanding which pages convert best can guide your content creation and link-building strategies. It's all about connecting the dots between search engine visibility and tangible results.

Effective conversion tracking is not just about gathering data but also about making informed decisions. Regularly reviewing your analytics, comparing time periods, and segmenting your audience can uncover trends and highlight opportunities for improvement. It's also beneficial to establish KPIs related to your business goals, so you remain focused on what truly matters. Consider running A/B tests on different elements of your site, from call-to-action buttons to page layouts, and measure the results. Remember, small tweaks can sometimes lead to significant improvements in conversion rates. By prioritizing conversion tracking and identifying user engagement metrics, you pave the way for long-term success in your digital marketing efforts.

12.5 Understanding Domain Authority (DA) and Page Authority (PA): Why They Are Pseudo Metrics

Domain Authority (DA) and Page Authority (PA) are scores developed by Moz to estimate a website's strength and ranking potential within search engine results. DA is a composite score that ranges from 1 to 100, with higher values indicating a greater likelihood of achieving favorable rankings. In contrast, PA evaluates the ranking potential of individual pages, focusing on the quality and quantity of inbound links. While DA encompasses all pages under a domain, PA offers a concentrated analysis of a specific page. Both metrics stem from a combination of factors, including total link counts and linking root domains.

It is essential to recognize that DA and PA are considered pseudo metrics, as they do not rely on direct data from Google. These scores are based on Moz's proprietary algorithm, offering a general overview of a site's performance rather than definitive insights into actual rankings. Nonetheless, they serve as helpful tools for benchmarking your website against competitors and identifying strengths and weaknesses within your SEO strategy.

By analyzing your DA and PA, you gain insight into your website's standing relative to others. If your DA falls short compared to competitors, it may signal a need to reassess your link-building and content strategies. Improving your domain authority often involves crafting high-quality content that naturally attracts backlinks and actively networking to secure additional links. PA helps you focus on specific pages; a high PA with low traffic may suggest that your content requires further promotion or optimization to reach a broader audience.

Regularly monitoring these metrics can reveal trends and shifts that inform your ongoing strategy. A practical approach is to maintain a spreadsheet that logs your DA and PA alongside those of competitors. This visual representation clarifies your progress and demonstrates how your SEO efforts are influencing your site's authority. By diligently tracking these metrics, you can make informed decisions, ensuring your SEO strategies remain effective and your online presence continues to thrive.

Chapter 13: Keeping Up with SEO Trends

13.1 The Ever-Changing Landscape of SEO

SEO is not a static entity; it evolves and shifts constantly in response to a variety of factors. As I delve into the world of search engine optimization, I realize that the strategies we deploy today may become obsolete tomorrow. Search engines like Google are continually updating their algorithms, aiming to provide users with the most relevant and valuable content. Keeping up with these changes is essential, and it requires us to be not just adaptive but proactive in our approach to SEO. The trends that shape SEO can stem from user behavior, technological advancements, and even societal shifts, so being aware of these dynamics can provide us with opportunities for better visibility.

Moreover, understanding how consumers seek information online has become increasingly important. Changes in user intent, mobile usage, and voice search are reshaping how we optimize our websites. For instance, more people are using voice search through their devices, which means we need to rethink our keywords and content structure to cater to conversational queries. This trend emphasizes the importance of being flexible and open to experimenting with different strategies as they emerge. The need for agility in SEO should not be underestimated; we must be willing to pivot and adjust our tactics in real-time as we monitor performance and insights.

A variety of factors are driving these changes, and recognizing them is crucial for anyone involved in digital marketing or web development. One major driving force is the advancement of technology. With the rise of AI and machine learning, search engines are becoming smarter and more intuitive. They are beginning to understand context and intent much better, allowing for more personalized search results. This means we should focus on creating high-quality, relevant content that truly addresses the needs of our audience, as generic SEO tactics will falter against more sophisticated algorithms.

User experience is another key element influencing SEO. Websites that load quickly and provide an enjoyable browsing experience are favored in search rankings. As webmasters and SEO specialists, we need to prioritize site speed, mobile optimization, and intuitive navigation to appeal to both users and search engines. Additionally, the continuous rise of social media metrics is affecting how search engines evaluate content. Engaging directly with our audience through platforms like Instagram or Twitter can boost our brand visibility and indirectly improve our SEO by increasing backlinks and driving traffic to our sites.

As we navigate this ever-changing landscape, one practical tip is to consistently monitor and analyze our SEO performance. Utilizing tools like Google Analytics and Search Console can help us identify trends, spot opportunities, and troubleshoot issues before they escalate. The more we understand our own data, the better equipped we'll be to adapt to this dynamic field.

13.2 Adapting to Algorithm Updates: What You Need to Know

Staying current with search engine algorithm updates is crucial for anyone involved in digital marketing, web development, or SEO. Search engines like Google frequently tweak their algorithms to provide users with the best possible results, which means our strategies need to evolve as well. If we ignore these updates, we risk losing visibility and traffic. Algorithms are designed to catch manipulative tactics and low-quality content, and if our websites don't align with these changes, we may find ourselves penalized. Being proactive in understanding these shifts ensures we maintain our rankings and reach our target audience effectively.

Adapting our SEO strategies in response to these updates requires a combination of flexibility and knowledge. Regularly reviewing keywords and content performance helps us identify which areas need adjustment. It's also essential to focus on high-quality content that provides real value to users. We should embrace a user-first mindset, focusing on enhancing the overall experience of visitors to our sites. Implementing structured data, improving page load speeds, and ensuring mobile compatibility are all crucial factors to consider. As algorithms increasingly prioritize user engagement metrics, we should pay close attention to how visitors interact with our content.

Stay informed by following SEO blogs, attending webinars, and participating in digital marketing forums. Engaging with the community allows us to share insights and gather tips on best practices related to recent updates. One practical strategy is to conduct regular audits of our website to pinpoint areas of improvement and assess how well our strategies align with the philosophy behind the latest algorithm changes. Consistently refining our approaches not only keeps us relevant but builds long-term credibility and trust with search engines and our audience alike.

13.3 Staying Ahead: Following Industry Experts

In the fast-evolving world of SEO, staying updated with the best practices and insights from top industry practitioners is crucial for success. Numerous resources are available where SEO experts share their knowledge. Blogs like Moz, Search Engine Journal, and Neil Patel's website are gold mines of information. They cover a wide array of topics from algorithm changes to link-building strategies, and they regularly feature content from seasoned professionals who have been in the industry for years. Podcasts are another fantastic way to glean insights. Shows like The SEJ Show and Marketing School host industry leaders who discuss the latest trends and answer listener questions. Additionally, platforms like Twitter and LinkedIn allow you to follow experts in real time, catching their thoughts on current events in the digital marketing landscape. Subscribing to newsletters is equally beneficial, delivering curated information directly to your inbox. These resources not only keep you informed but also expose you to diverse perspectives and strategies that can enhance your own work.

Engaging with experts and being part of the SEO community can greatly enrich your experience and learning curve. Joining forums, such as the Moz Community or Reddit's SEO subreddit, opens up a world of networking where you can ask questions, share knowledge, and connect with fellow enthusiasts and professionals. Don't hesitate to participate in discussions or present your insights; it's a great way to make your voice heard. Attending SEO conferences and webinars also provides an excellent opportunity to learn directly from leaders in the field. Events like SMX and Pubcon allow you to interact with speakers, attend workshops, and meet like-minded individuals who share your passion for SEO. On social media, engaging with experts by commenting on their posts or sharing their content not only expands your network but can also attract their attention—sometimes leading to direct conversations, mentorship opportunities, or even collaboration on projects. Remember, building connections within the community can open many doors.

To truly benefit from following industry experts, make sure to actively apply what you learn. It's not just about absorbing information but integrating new strategies into your own SEO practices. Start a blog or a personal project where you can experiment with the insights and techniques discussed by the experts you follow. Document your journey, share your findings within the community, and be open to feedback. This will not only deepen your understanding but also solidify your identity as a knowledgeable player in the field. Embrace a mindset of continuous learning and share your takeaways, as this will further strengthen relationships with industry leaders and fellow professionals alike.

13.4 Continuous Learning and Adaptation

To stay relevant in the fast-evolving world of SEO, ongoing education has become an essential part of our daily routine. The digital landscape changes quickly, with search engine algorithms frequently updated and new trends emerging all the time. This means that what worked six months ago might be outdated today. By committing to continuous learning, we not only keep our skills sharp but also gain a competitive edge. It allows us to experiment with new strategies, tools, and techniques while avoiding common pitfalls that can arise from outdated knowledge. The SEO community is filled with resources like webinars, online courses, and blogs that keep us informed about the latest developments. Participating in these learning opportunities helps us adapt our tactics to meet current demands and ultimately improves the performance of our websites.

Building a culture of learning in your marketing team opens up avenues for innovation and creativity. Encouraging team members to share insights from their individual learning experiences fosters an environment where everyone can grow. Weekly knowledge-sharing sessions can be effective, allowing each person to present something they've learned recently. This not only reinforces their own understanding but also benefits the entire team. Nurturing curiosity is key; offering access to courses and encouraging attendance at industry conferences can amplify the team's collective knowledge. As we empower our team to seek out learning opportunities, we create a stronger, more adaptable unit, capable of navigating the complexities of our field with ease. Additionally, embracing failures as learning moments can lead to valuable insights and ultimately propel the team's success.

Incorporating learning goals as part of performance reviews can also serve to emphasize the importance of ongoing education. It keeps everyone accountable and motivated to enhance their skills. This focus on learning is not just beneficial for individual growth but solidifies the team's ability to tackle challenges together. When everyone is aligned with a shared goal of continuous education, we build resilience and adaptability into our team dynamic, ensuring we can meet whatever challenges the SEO landscape throws our way.

Chapter 14: Common SEO Mistakes to Avoid

14.1 Ignoring Mobile Users: Is it a Big Mistake

Neglecting mobile optimization can have serious consequences that often go unnoticed. As webmasters and digital marketers, we may focus predominantly on desktop users, overlooking the vast number of individuals accessing the internet via mobile devices. This oversight can result in a fragmented user experience. Pages lacking mobile optimization may load slowly, feature cumbersome navigation, and present content that is difficult to read on smaller screens. As a consequence, potential customers may abandon their searches in favor of competitors who offer superior mobile experiences. More importantly, disregarding mobile users can negatively impact your site's SEO rankings, as search engines increasingly emphasize mobile-friendliness in their algorithms. This neglect can lead to reduced visibility in search results and ultimately fewer conversions, undermining your efforts and potentially affecting your bottom line.

Adopting a mobile-first strategy is not merely a trend; it is essential in today's digital landscape. By prioritizing mobile optimization, we can enhance user engagement significantly. A mobile-friendly site ensures that content is not only accessible but also enjoyable and easy to navigate. With intuitive layouts and fast loading times, optimizing for mobile fosters a seamless experience that encourages users to engage more deeply with our content. Enhanced engagement often translates into higher conversion rates, as satisfied users become customers willing to take action—whether that's making a purchase, signing up for a newsletter, or sharing their experience on social media. By focusing on mobile users, we can cultivate a stronger connection with our audience and improve the overall effectiveness of our marketing strategies.

Moreover, understanding your specific audience's needs is crucial.

Are they looking for quick information or in-depth content? Is their primary goal entertainment or purchase? Analyzing user behavior on mobile devices can provide insights that inform your strategy, allowing you to tailor your offerings appropriately. It is important to remember that not all mobile traffic is low-quality. In fact, a well-optimized site can attract highly engaged users who are more likely to convert. By treating mobile users as a priority rather than an afterthought, you can leverage this traffic effectively, enhancing not just your SEO but your brand's reputation in the marketplace.

A practical tip for enhancing mobile optimization is to regularly test your site on different devices. Tools like Google's Mobile-Friendly Test offer valuable insights into your site's mobile performance. Conducting these regular checks and updates will ensure that you adapt to evolving user behaviors, keeping your site's performance optimal and your audience engaged. Staying ahead of mobile trends not only strengthens your current user base but also positions your brand competitively for the future.

14.2 Keyword Stuffing: Why It Backfires

Keyword stuffing refers to the practice of cramming a multitude of keywords into your content with the hope of ranking higher on search engines. While this tactic might seem like a shortcut to improving visibility, it invariably leads to several pitfalls. First, it dilutes the quality of the content, making it challenging for readers to engage with what you've written. Instead of creating value, you're creating confusion. Readers can quickly recognize when a piece of content is written primarily for search engines rather than for them, leading to an immediate disconnect. The result? Increased bounce rates as users navigate away in search of more meaningful and coherent information.

Additionally, keyword stuffing can severely hamper your efforts to establish credibility. In a world where genuine content is highly valued, audiences are becoming savvier and prefer authentic, valuable information. Therefore, when they encounter keyword-heavy content that lacks depth or insight, they tend to view the author—and the associated brand—as untrustworthy. Over time, this can damage your reputation, making it harder to build an audience or community of loyal readers. What began as a quick fix for visibility could turn into a long-term setback, ultimately hindering your growth as a digital marketer or webmaster.

User experience is a crucial factor that can make or break a website's success. When content is stuffed with keywords, it often sacrifices simplicity and clarity. Instead of seamless navigation through well-crafted, informative text, users find themselves slogging through a repetitive maze of keywords. This may also lead to frustration, as users have to decipher what the content is truly about among the clutter. They want to feel understood and valued, not tricked into clicking through a page just to be met with overwhelming jargon and repeated phrases that provide little to no actual information.

14.3 Neglecting User Experience: The Hidden Cost

Neglecting user experience can be a costly mistake for webmasters and digital marketers alike. User experience (UX) plays a crucial role in determining how visitors interact with your website. When users land on a site that is confusing or difficult to navigate, they are likely to leave quickly, leading to high bounce rates. Search engines like Google take these metrics into account when ranking websites. A poor user experience can result in lower search engine rankings, decreased organic traffic, and ultimately, a negative impact on your business. By enhancing user experience, not only are you improving usability for your visitors, but you're also signaling to search engines that your site is valuable and trustworthy.

To create a seamless user experience, it's vital to focus on aspects such as page load speed, mobile optimization, and intuitive navigation. When your pages load slowly, users are impatient and might abandon the site before it even fully loads. Similarly, with the rise of mobile browsing, having a responsive design that caters to various screen sizes is essential. Non-responsive websites often frustrate users, forcing them to seek information elsewhere. Therefore, understanding the connection between user experience and SEO is the first step toward optimizing your website for better performance in search results.

Improving user experience involves implementing a variety of strategies that cater to your audience's needs and preferences. Start by ensuring that your website's design is clean and user-friendly. Clear calls to action, simple layouts, and easily accessible information make it easier for visitors to navigate your site and find what they're looking for. Consider conducting user testing to gather feedback on your site's usability. This input can be valuable for identifying pain points and areas for improvement.

Content plays a significant role in enhancing user experience as well. Providing valuable, engaging, and relevant content keeps visitors on your site longer. Use headings, bullet points, and images to break up text and make it more digestible. Also, incorporate multimedia elements like videos and infographics to enrich the experience. Offering a search function can also help users find specific content quickly, further improving their overall experience.

Ultimately, regular performance assessments of your website will help you identify areas needing attention. Tools like Google Analytics provide insights into user behavior, helping you understand where visitors are dropping off and what they're engaging with the most. By continually refining the user experience on your website, you not only create a more enjoyable environment for your visitors but also boost your site's SEO performance.

As a practical tip, always keep the user journey in mind. When making design or content decisions, ask yourself how it will impact the user's experience. This perspective can guide you toward creating a website that satisfies both users and search engines.

Chapter 15: Case Studies in Successful SEO

15.1 Small Businesses That Transformed with SEO, Two Examples

Real-life examples of small businesses leveraging SEO successfully can be found in every corner of the digital landscape. One notable case is a small local bakery named Sweet Crumbs. When they first launched their website, they were barely getting any traffic, and their lovely pastries remained a hidden gem in the community. They realized that despite having an appealing website, they weren't reaching their desired audience. By investing in SEO, particularly through local search optimization, they began to appear in search results when people looked for bakeries in the area. Through keyword research focused on locality and bakery-related terms, they transformed their online presence, ultimately leading to an increase in storefront traffic and sales. Another inspiring example is a small eco-friendly cleaning supplies company called Green Shine. They recognized the need to stand out in a saturated market. By implementing SEO strategies such as content marketing, they created informative blog posts about sustainability and cleaning tips. These posts not only educated their audience but also helped their website rank higher in search engine results. Consequently, their site saw a significant uptick in visitors, and they established themselves as a go-to resource in the eco-friendly niche.

The key strategies that led to their transformation were rooted in understanding their target audience and optimizing their online presence accordingly. For Sweet Crumbs, incorporating local SEO tactics such as claiming their Google My Business listing and encouraging happy customers to leave positive reviews made a remarkable difference. They also used local keywords throughout their website and blog content, which led to higher visibility in local searches. For Green Shine, focusing on quality content was paramount. They prioritized creating blogs that not only featured their products but also sparked conversations about eco-friendly living. This content strategy paired with strong social media marketing allowed them to engage users beyond the transactional space. They also utilized backlinks from reputable blogs and websites in the green living community, which significantly boosted their domain authority and search rankings.

Both examples highlight the importance of an adaptive and audience-focused approach in SEO. Sweet Crumbs and Green Shine did not shy away from experimenting with different strategies, which is crucial in the ever-evolving digital landscape. One practical tip for webmasters, digital marketers, and SEO specialists is to never underestimate the power of content tailored to your audience's interests and needs. Regularly update your website with relevant content that answers questions your potential customers may have, and always keep an eye on the latest SEO trends. This not only enhances your visibility but also establishes your brand as an authority in your niche.

15.2 Learning from Failed SEO Campaigns, Two Examples

In my experience, analyzing failed SEO campaigns is one of the most enlightening exercises a digital marketer can undertake. I recall two cases where the intentions were good but execution lacked the needed finesse, leading to disappointing outcomes. The first case involved a reputable e-commerce site that decided to launch a major SEO overhaul to improve its rankings. They rushed into the project, failing to conduct a thorough keyword analysis. Instead of targeting terms that would actually attract their desired customer base, they optimized for popular but highly competitive keywords with little relevance to their products. As a result, even after months of effort, they noticed negligible traffic increase and poor conversion rates, highlighting the importance of aligning keywords with customer intent.

The second case was a local service provider who aimed to increase visibility through local SEO. They invested significantly in building backlinks and creating content, all without fully optimizing their Google My Business listing. Despite their efforts in content and outreach, they remained invisible on local search results because they neglected fundamental local SEO practices. The lesson here is clear: no matter how much effort you put into certain aspects of SEO, overlooking the basics can lead to failure. For both campaigns, the common thread was a misalignment between their strategies and the practical necessities of SEO, resulting in wasted resources and missed opportunities.

From these experiences, I learned the critical importance of a structured approach to SEO. It's essential to start with comprehensive research and a clear understanding of objectives. Always prioritize foundational elements, such as keyword relevance and local listing optimization, before diving into more complex strategies. Managing expectations is also vital; SEO is not an overnight phenomenon but a sustained effort. A practical tip would be to regularly audit your strategies and continuously educate yourself and your team about the evolving SEO landscape. This can help prevent you from falling into the traps that others have navigated and ensure that your campaigns are on the right path.

15.3 Innovative SEO Strategies That Worked, Three Examples

Throughout my journey in digital marketing, I've observed a number of unique SEO strategies that truly stand out due to their innovative approaches and remarkable results. One notable case involved a small e-commerce website that shifted its focus from broad keywords to long-tail keywords that specifically addressed niche markets. By creating highly detailed product pages that aligned closely with those long-tail keywords, they drew in highly targeted traffic, which significantly boosted their conversion rates. Another example is from a local service provider that utilized customer-generated content through reviews and testimonials. They encouraged happy clients to share their positive experiences on social media and their website, which not only improved SEO because of the fresh, unique content, but also enhanced trust with potential customers. Lastly, a tech blog I followed experimented with interactive content, such as quizzes and calculators, which not only kept users engaged but also attracted backlinks from other sites wanting to share these interactive pieces. This strategy led to a substantial increase in organic traffic as Google recognized the valuable user engagement. Each of these strategies highlighted a keen understanding of audience needs and innovative thinking that defied conventional norms in the industry.

When breaking down these tactics, several key takeaways can inspire your future SEO efforts. The first lesson is the power of specificity. Focus on long-tail keywords that cater to your target audience's unique needs, as this not only helps you rank better but also attracts users with a higher likelihood of converting. The second takeaway is the invaluable role of social proof. Encouraging existing customers to share their experiences online can create a buzz around your brand, enhance your credibility, and produce fresh content that search engines crave. Cultivating a base of reviews can lead to better visibility in local searches, emphasizing the idea that trust is as critical to SEO as technical configurations. Lastly, don't shy away from interactive elements in your content strategy. Engaging users through quizzes, tools, or interactive infographics can significantly boost user retention and lower bounce rates, making your site appealing to search engines. By blending creativity with an understanding of your audience's needs, you can develop SEO strategies that not only elevate your search rankings but also foster long-term engagement.

Remember to constantly analyze the performance of your strategies using tools like Google Analytics and adjust accordingly. SEO is not static, and what works today might need refining tomorrow. Stay curious and open to experimentation, as adapting to trends and shifting consumer behaviors is the key to maintaining relevance in the ever-evolving digital landscape.

Chapter 16: White Hat SEO vs Black Hat SEO

16.1 SEO Strategies Unveiled: The Ethical Divide Between White Hat and Black Hat SEO

White hat SEO refers to the practices that adhere to search engine guidelines, focusing on creating a sustainable and organic online presence. These strategies emphasize high-quality content, keyword research, and user experience, aiming to engage real audiences genuinely. On the other hand, black hat SEO employs techniques that prioritize quick results over ethical considerations. This approach often includes tactics like keyword stuffing, cloaking, and buying backlinks, which can lead to penalties from search engines. The defining factor between the two lies in their intent; while white hat strategies build long-term relationships with users and search engines, black hat tactics aim for immediate gains by circumventing rules.

The implications of these approaches on brand reputation are significant. Brands that engage in white hat SEO generally find that their commitment to ethical practices earns them trust and loyalty from their audience. This trust translates into higher engagement and conversion rates and encourages positive word-of-mouth marketing. Conversely, brands that rely on black hat techniques risk severe reputational damage. If a company is caught using black hat SEO, it can face penalties like being de-indexed from search engine results, severely limiting its visibility. Furthermore, being labeled as an unethical brand can deter potential customers and partners, making recovery a long and challenging process. The choice between these two paths isn't simply a matter of strategy; it significantly affects how a brand is perceived in the marketplace.

Understanding the landscape of white hat and black hat SEO can help you make more informed decisions about your digital marketing strategies. At the end of the day, the choice you make will reflect your brand's values and influence your long-term success in the digital world. Consider focusing on building genuine relationships with your audience through valuable content and ethical practices, ensuring that your SEO efforts align with a sustainable and successful brand strategy.

16.2 The Dark Side of SEO: What Is Black Hat SEO and Why Should You Avoid It?

Black hat SEO techniques may seem like a quick shortcut to ranking higher on search engines, but they carry significant risks that can jeopardize your website's visibility and reputation. These practices often violate search engine guidelines, leading to potential penalties. When you engage in black hat tactics like keyword stuffing, cloaking, or buying backlinks, you're essentially playing with fire. One wrong move can result in your site being deindexed or facing a dramatic drop in rankings. This not only impacts traffic but can also lead to a loss of revenue, especially for businesses that rely heavily on online visibility. Furthermore, employing these tactics can damage your brand's credibility. When users discover that you've employed underhanded strategies, trust can be shattered, pushing potential customers away. The investment in black hat SEO may yield short-term gains, but the long-term consequences can haunt you for years to come.

Real-life examples of penalties faced by black hat practitioners often serve as cautionary tales. Take, for instance, the case of a well-known e-commerce site that resorted to spammy link-building tactics. Initially, they saw a surge in traffic and sales, but not long after, they faced a manual penalty from Google. Their site dropped from a top position to almost invisible, with revenue plummeting by nearly 80%. In another instance, a digital marketing agency thought it could outsmart Google by creating mirrored sites with duplicated content. This attempt at trickery led to a complete ban from search results, essentially rendering their hard work pointless. These examples emphasize the unpredictability of the algorithm and the swift punishment that can follow unethical practices. When you weigh the risks against potential rewards, the gamble of black hat practices is hardly worth it.

16.3 Gray Hat Tactics for SEO: Navigating the Risky And Punishing Territory, Gray Hat SEO Explained

Gray hat SEO occupies that peculiar middle ground between the white hat approaches that adhere strictly to search engine guidelines and the black hat tactics that aim to manipulate search rankings through dubious means. Understanding these gray hat strategies becomes critical for webmasters and digital marketers who want to improve their site's visibility without crossing the line into territory that could lead to penalties. Examples of gray hat tactics might include the use of clickbait titles, buying expired domains, or manipulating review systems in subtle ways. While these techniques stop short of outright deceit, they often play within the margins, and their distinction can feel like a blurry line. They may not consistently align with best practices, yet many find their potential for bringing quick results undeniable.

However, with any gray hat strategy comes a hefty dose of risk. Engaging in such tactics can lead to temporary gains but often carries the shadow of consequences from search engines, including penalties that can devalue a site or even lead to its removal from search results. The benefits can be enticing: improved rankings, higher traffic, and better conversions. Yet, the repercussions can be severe, both in terms of traffic drops and loss of reputation. It's crucial to assess your business's risk tolerance. Some might navigate this area with success, becoming savvy in not getting caught, while others may find the backlash insurmountable. It's about weighing the short-term benefits against the long-term viability and sustainability of the strategies employed.

As you strategize your approach to gray hat SEO, consider developing a clear set of principles to differentiate between safe experimentation and reckless behavior. Educating yourself on recent algorithm updates and understanding the evolving SEO landscape can bolster your efforts. Making data-driven decisions based on performance metrics can provide insight into what works and what might risk your site's health. A practical tip for anyone delving into gray hat methods is to maintain transparency with your audience. Building trust with users only strengthens your digital presence and can provide a safety net should any tactics fall under scrutiny.

16.4 Top White Hat SEO Techniques to Improve Your Site's Authority and Trust

Building authority online is much more than just a trendy buzzword. It's about gaining recognition as a reliable, respected source in your niche. One of the most effective white hat techniques to achieve this is through consistently creating high-quality content that resonates with your audience. When you provide valuable insights, tutorials, or compelling stories, your users are more likely to trust your brand. By focusing on the needs and interests of your target audience, you encourage organic sharing and engagement. This not only enhances your reach but also builds your reputation over time.

Another cornerstone of establishing authority is participating in relevant online communities. Whether it's through comments on blogs, engaging in forums, or sharing expertise on social media, being an active and helpful member of your niche can significantly increase your credibility. Professionals appreciate collaboration, so seek out opportunities to guest post or collaborate with influencers. This not only exposes you to new audiences but also associates you with established names in your field, effectively transferring some of their authority to you.

Trust is a delicate balance that takes time to build, and it requires consistent effort. One effective long-term strategy is transparency. Being open about your business practices, your sources, and your methodologies can weave a fabric of trust that becomes your safety net during challenging times. For instance, openly discussing why you choose to work with certain tools or platforms can demystify your process and connect with your audience on a more personal level.

Moreover, ensuring that your website is user-friendly and offers a seamless experience is crucial. A well-structured site, with fast load times and easy navigation, reflects professionalism and reliability, two qualities that directly impact trust. Additionally, collecting and showcasing testimonials and reviews can be a powerful tool. When potential clients see positive feedback from others, it acts as social proof, reinforcing your credibility. Always encourage happy customers to leave reviews, as each positive word strengthens the fabric of trust you're building.

Remember, trust and authority are not built overnight, but by implementing these strategies and consistently prioritizing your audience's needs, you will lay a strong foundation for lasting relationships. Engaging with your audience through regular updates, newsletters, or blog posts can keep the conversation going and further solidify your status as a trusted authority in your field.

16.5 Top 5 Black Hat SEO Techniques to Watch Out For

There are a few common black hat techniques every marketer should avoid if they want their websites to flourish. Keyword stuffing, for instance, is when someone crams a webpage with a single keyword or phrase, hoping to trick search engines into ranking their page higher. This not only creates a poor user experience but can also lead to penalties. Another technique is cloaking, where the content presented to search engines differs from what users see. Webmasters who engage in this deceptive practice risk severe consequences, including being banned from search results. Other tactics include the use of private link networks, where webmasters buy links from sites that exist solely to pass authority, and duplicate content, where the same content appears on multiple domains in an effort to manipulate search rankings. Finally, there's the practice of creating doorway pages, which are low-quality pages designed to rank for specific keywords but yield little value for visitors. Each of these tactics might seem tempting in the short term, but they can jeopardize a website's credibility and visibility over time.

Identifying these harmful tactics is crucial to safeguard your website and maintain its integrity. Always take a close look at your website's analytics and performance metrics. If you notice significant drops in rankings or traffic, it could signal the use of black hat techniques, either by yourself or competitors. Familiarizing yourself with your site's content and backlink profile can also alert you to any red flags. Regular audits can help ensure compliance with search engine guidelines. Implementing automated tools designed to detect issues related to SEO practices can streamline this process, making it easier to spot anything suspicious before it negatively impacts your rankings. Additionally, engaging in transparent and ethical SEO practices by focusing on quality content, user experience, and legitimate ways to earn backlinks ultimately promotes long-term growth and success.

It's vital to remember that the digital landscape is always evolving, and search engines are getting smarter. Staying informed about the latest SEO trends and best practices can help you protect your website from harmful tactics. One practical tip is to cultivate a robust network of professionals in the SEO community. Networking allows for knowledge sharing and provides insights into both effective strategies and potential threats looming in the industry. This proactive approach not only enhances your understanding of SEO but also equips you to defend against black hat techniques that could jeopardize your efforts.

Chapter 17: The Future of SEO

17.1 Voice Search and Its Impact on SEO

Voice search has become a powerful tool for users seeking information quickly and effortlessly. With the increasing popularity of smart speakers and mobile assistants like Siri, Google Assistant, and Alexa, the way we approach SEO is changing significantly. People tend to speak differently than they type; they ask questions in a more conversational tone, which directly affects how we should structure our content. This shift toward voice-activated search means that webmasters and SEO specialists need to rethink their strategies. Instead of focusing solely on keywords, we should emphasize long-tail phrases and natural language. By understanding the patterns of speech that users employ when querying voice search systems, we can better align our content to match their needs.

Search engines are increasingly prioritizing content that answers specific questions, providing valuable insights directly to users. Therefore, utilizing a question-and-answer format in your content can enhance its chances of being featured in voice search results. Also, the prominence of local search through voice queries cannot be overlooked, as many users search for nearby services or businesses using voice commands. This reality reinforces the necessity for optimized local SEO strategies, including maintaining accurate business listings and engaging in local link building, which can elevate your visibility on voice search platforms.

To effectively cater to voice search, it's crucial to create content that is not only informative but also easily digestible for voice-activated devices. This involves crafting concise answers and breaking down complex ideas into simple, straightforward language. Additionally, implementing structured data can greatly assist search engines in understanding the context of your content, enhancing its chances of being pulled into voice search responses. Utilizing schema markup aids in providing the necessary clues for search engines to categorize your content correctly, thus making it more accessible through voice queries.

Furthermore, optimizing your site for mobile is essential, as a significant portion of voice searches is conducted on smartphones. A responsive design ensures that users can access your content seamlessly, regardless of the device they use. As you adapt your strategies for voice search, consider incorporating more visual content, such as images and video, as these often complement spoken queries effectively. Remember, the ultimate goal is to provide valuable answers to your audience, making your content not only accessible but also engaging. As voice search continues to evolve, keeping your content frequently updated will help maintain your competitive advantage.

Integrating these tactics will not only enhance your site's performance in voice search but also contribute to an improved overall user experience. Pay attention to analytics to refine your approach continually; track voice search traffic and behavioral patterns to adjust your content strategy, ensuring you are always ahead of the curve.

17.2 The Rising Importance of Video Content

Video content has rapidly transformed the digital landscape, becoming a crucial element for search engine optimization (SEO). This shift is largely driven by user behavior—people are naturally drawn to visual content, and statistics clearly reflect this trend. When users search online, they are not only looking for text-based information but also for engaging, meaningful visuals that can convey information more effectively. This makes video content a powerful tool that can significantly increase your website's visibility on search engines.

Search engines, particularly Google, are evolving to prioritize video content because they recognize that users enjoy and benefit from it. Videos can lead to longer site visits and lower bounce rates, which are positive signals for SEO ranking. Moreover, a well-optimized video can appear in search results, Google's Featured Snippets, or even as a rich result, putting your content in front of a larger audience. Understanding this importance can help webmasters, digital marketers, and SEO specialists leverage video as a strategic asset in their content marketing efforts.

To truly harness the power of video for SEO, optimization is key. Start with choosing video titles that are engaging and keyword-rich. The title should not only grab attention but also accurately represent what's in the video. Additionally, using concise, informative descriptions packed with relevant keywords can help search engines understand the video's context. Creating engaging thumbnails can also entice viewers to click and improve your video's click-through rate (CTR).

It's also important to provide transcripts for your video content. This not only enhances accessibility but also gives search engines more text to crawl, which can improve SEO outcomes. Implementing structured data, such as schema markup, can further assist search engines in indexing your content properly. Ensure videos load quickly and are mobile-friendly, as page speed and user experience are critical ranking factors. Finally, sharing your videos on social media platforms can drive traffic back to your site, enhancing your SEO presence. Remember, every element counts in creating a holistic approach to video optimization.

Incorporating video into your overall content strategy isn't just a trend but brings tangible benefits for SEO and audience engagement. By understanding how to effectively use and optimize video content, you can elevate your digital presence and connect more deeply with your audience.

17.3 Anticipating Changes in User Behavior

User behavior is not static; it continually evolves due to various factors, including technological advancements, shifting societal values, and changes in consumer preferences. Understanding these behavioral shifts can be a game-changer for anyone involved in SEO. For instance, the rise of mobile devices transformed how users search for information, leading to the necessity for mobile-optimized sites. As webmasters and digital marketers, we must stay attuned to these trends to ensure our strategies align with users' needs. Regularly analyzing user data and staying updated on industry reports can help in predicting upcoming trends. If we can anticipate these changes, we can adapt our content strategies effectively, making sure we remain visible to our target audience.

To thrive in an environment where user behavior can shift overnight, being proactive is essential. This means not just reacting to changes but also preparing for them before they happen. One effective strategy is to foster a culture of continuous learning within your team. Engaging with tools that provide insights into user engagement and developing a flexible content calendar can be instrumental. For instance, if data suggests a growing interest in sustainability, pivoting your content to include eco-friendly practices and products can position you favorably. Collaborating with influencers who resonate with this trend can further enhance your visibility. Embracing versatility in our approaches not only helps in staying ahead of the curve but also builds trust and credibility with our audiences. Remember, staying ahead in SEO is not about following the trends but creating them based on what you anticipate users will seek.

Ultimately, maintaining an adaptive mindset ensures you're not merely reacting to changes but proactively shaping them, leading to a more resilient SEO strategy. Keeping an eye on emerging technologies and trends can provide insights into how people will interact with content in the future, ensuring that our strategies remain relevant and effective.

17.4 Will Oldschool Internet Survive, Blogs, Content Hubs and Similar Platforms

The longevity of traditional internet platforms, like blogs and content hubs, is a fascinating topic that many of us in the digital space have been pondering. As the internet evolves rapidly, with new technologies and platforms continuously emerging, it's easy to question whether these older formats can survive. However, if we look closely at their fundamental nature, we notice that they provide something unique. Blogs and content hubs are often built around deep engagement, meaningful content, and personal expression, which resonate well with audiences. Unlike the fast-paced consumption of social media, these platforms allow for deeper dives into topics that matter to users. This characteristic is essential, especially as audiences become increasingly disillusioned with the superficiality often found on newer platforms. Moreover, search engines continue to prioritize quality content, which works in favor of blogs and dedicated content hubs. They can remain relevant by adapting their strategies—focusing on SEO, enriching user experience, and offering unique insights that cannot be found elsewhere.

Looking toward the future, there are numerous opportunities for blogs and content hubs to thrive. With the increasing value placed on authenticity and trust, well-established blogs can capitalize on this shift by fostering genuine connections with their audiences. Building communities around niche topics can enhance user loyalty and engagement. Furthermore, the rise of multimedia content is another avenue. Incorporating video, podcasts, and interactive elements can transform a standard blog into a vibrant content hub that appeals to a broader audience. The integration of e-commerce into blogs presents another opportunity; many readers appreciate the convenience of discovering products related to their interests without leaving the site. Additionally, brands look to collaborate with content creators who genuinely resonate with their values, paving the way for partnership opportunities. Staying innovative while keeping the core values of authenticity and audience engagement will be crucial for blogs and content hubs in navigating the ever-changing digital landscape.

Overall, the survival of these platforms hinges on their adaptability. To thrive, webmasters, digital marketers, and SEO specialists should focus on continuous learning, staying updated with current trends, and understanding their audience's evolving needs. Engaging your community and providing valuable, comprehensive content can distinguish your platform. Don't hesitate to experiment with new formats and technologies while remaining true to the purpose that led you to create your blog or content hub in the first place.

17.5 Will AI Replace it All

...or it Will Lead to New Golden Ages and a new beginning of Blogging and Content Creation

Examining the potential of AI to evolve content creation and marketing shows us fascinating possibilities. The integration of AI in content production can enhance productivity, allowing writers and marketers to focus on creativity rather than tedious tasks. AI tools can help generate topic ideas, write drafts, and even suggest SEO enhancements tailored to specific keywords. This not only streamlines the workflow but also enables webmasters and digital marketers to produce high-quality content that resonates with their target audience. AI's capability to analyze vast data sets can lead to more personalized content, making it relevant and engaging for individual users. As we embrace these tools, it's essential to maintain human oversight to ensure authenticity and connection with readers, which is something AI cannot replicate fully.

Speculations on the future landscape of blogging with AI advancements reveal a more collaborative approach. Instead of replacing human bloggers, AI will likely serve as a powerful partner in the content creation process. We might see a surge in blogs and articles that integrate AI insights, providing deeper analyses and perspectives that would take humans much longer to produce. Advanced algorithms could even help create dynamic content, adjusting in real-time based on reader preferences and behavior. This progression could spark a new golden age of blogging, where content is not only personalized but also enriched with in-depth research and data-driven insights. As digital marketers, understanding these advancements could help us redefine strategies and create engaging experiences that captivate our audiences.

As we look ahead, the key to thriving in this evolving landscape is adaptability. Embracing AI tools can enhance our workflow and allow us to explore innovative content strategies. However, it is crucial to strike a balance, ensuring that the human touch remains at the forefront of our work. Consider experimenting with AI applications, not just to save time but to inspire new ideas and approaches to storytelling. This could be the beginning of a new era in content creation—one where creativity and technology work hand in hand to produce exceptional content.

17.6 How Does Use of AI Has an Explosion of Potential, and a burst of possibilities

Implementing AI technology into SEO practices can feel like unlocking a treasure chest of opportunities. Machine learning algorithms sift through mountains of data in real-time, analyzing patterns that are often invisible to human eyes. For instance, AI can evaluate user behavior and engagement metrics, identifying which pages keep visitors hooked and which ones send them packing. This insight allows webmasters to optimize content based on actual user interaction rather than guesswork.

Moreover, AI tools can automate keyword research, revealing trending topics and long-tail keywords that capture user intent more effectively. Imagine having a personal assistant to crunch the numbers, ensuring that your strategies are continually tuned to the latest search engine algorithms. What's more, these tools can predict emerging trends based on historical data, allowing SEO specialists to pivot quickly and stay ahead of the competition. The cumulative effect is a streamlined process that not only saves time but also consistently delivers higher search rankings.

The marketing landscape is evolving rapidly, thanks to AI's entry into the arena. Chatbots powered by AI are transforming customer interactions, providing 24/7 support and personalized recommendations based on user inquiries. Through deep learning, these bots can understand tone and context, making their responses feel remarkably human-like, which enhances customer satisfaction and retention. Additionally, AI algorithms can analyze vast datasets to segment audiences more accurately than traditional methods, ensuring that campaigns reach the right people at the right time.

Another exciting application is predictive analytics. AI can forecast customer behavior based on historical data and current trends, which means marketers can proactively design campaigns that resonate with their audience's future preferences. Companies are using AI to create dynamic content that adapts to user interactions in real-time— think of personalized landing pages or customized product recommendations that evolve as user preferences shift. By leveraging these innovative strategies, digital marketers can not only amplify engagement but also drive conversions like never before.

As a practical takeaway, consider integrating AI tools into your strategy gradually. Begin with an area that seems most promising— perhaps automating keyword research or implementing a chatbot. Track the impact on your performance metrics and then expand from there. This way, you'll not only harness AI's power but also gain firsthand experience that will be invaluable as the technology continues to evolve.

Here are 50 advanced and unique ChatGPT prompts tailored for your SEO efforts

Here are **50 advanced and unique ChatGPT prompts** tailored for **SEO professionals** to perform **keyword research, clustering, competitive analysis, and strategy development**, modeled after your example. These are divided into strategic sections for clarity and usability:

Example: "Analyze the content of [competitor's website URL] and identify the primary and secondary keywords they are targeting."

🔍 Keyword Discovery & Expansion

1. "Generate a list of long-tail keywords in the '[your industry]' niche with search volume over 1000 and keyword difficulty under 30."

2. "Find informational keywords for '[topic]' that can be used in blog posts to drive top-of-funnel traffic."

3. "Suggest 25 keyword opportunities for '[service/product]' that are underserved by existing content."

4. "Provide keyword ideas for '[niche]' targeting voice search and virtual assistants like Alexa and Google Assistant."

5. "Generate seasonal keyword trends for '[industry]' based on historical Google Trends data."

6. "Identify keywords with rising interest in the '[topic]' niche over the past 12 months."

7. "List keyword opportunities for '[your niche]' that align with the E-E-A-T framework (Experience, Expertise, Authority, Trust)."

8. "Generate keywords around '[topic]' optimized for FAQ sections to increase organic visibility."

9. "Suggest keywords that combine '[main keyword]' with local modifiers for regional SEO."

10. "Find pain-point keywords that customers use when looking for solutions in the '[industry]' sector."

💡 Keyword Clustering, Mapping & Intent

11. "Cluster these keywords into awareness, consideration, and decision stages: [insert keywords]."

12. "Map these keywords to specific landing pages on an e-commerce website: [insert keywords]."

13. "Organize this keyword list into blog content silos to build topical authority: [insert keywords]."

14. "Suggest content formats (e.g., how-to, comparison, review) for each of these keywords based on intent: [insert keywords]."

15. "Break down the buyer journey for '[main keyword]' and provide keyword ideas for each stage."

16. "Group these keywords based on shared searcher intent and suggest a content calendar: [insert list]."

17. "Map keywords to a B2B SaaS website structure, covering homepage, features, blog, and support pages."

18. "Analyze these 10 keywords and classify them as informational, navigational, or transactional: [insert keywords]."

19. "Suggest semantically related keywords to '[topic]' for optimizing supporting content and improving relevance."

20. "Create a content funnel using keyword clusters based on these core terms: [insert keywords]."

💡 Competitive Keyword Intelligence

21. "Analyze '[competitor domain]' and list 20 keywords they rank for that you can target with better content."

22. "Compare the keyword profiles of '[your domain]' vs '[competitor domain]' and highlight gaps and opportunities."

23. "Identify low-difficulty keywords that top-ranking pages for '[keyword]' are missing."

24. "Analyze '[competitor domain]' for keywords driving traffic to their blog and suggest how to outperform them."

25. "Find keywords that multiple competitors rank for but your domain does not – suggest content to fill the gap."

26. "Suggest untapped long-tail keyword opportunities based on competitor backlink profiles."

27. "Analyze keywords where '[competitor]' ranks in positions 5–20 and recommend optimization strategies to outrank them."

28. "Identify keyword cannibalization issues in '[competitor domain]' and how to avoid them."

29. "Extract keyword opportunities from the most linked content on '[competitor domain]'."

30. "List keywords your competitor ranks for in Google Images, YouTube, or other vertical search engines."

⚡ SERP & Trend Optimization

31. "Analyze the SERP for '[keyword]' and list all the features (e.g., PAA, snippets, video results, maps)."

32. "Identify keywords that trigger video results and suggest content ideas for YouTube SEO."

33. "Find keywords with high CTR potential based on current SERP layouts for '[topic]'."

34. "Suggest keyword opportunities in '[niche]' that appear in 'People Also Ask' results frequently."

35. "List keywords with featured snippet opportunities and suggest how to structure content to win them."

36. "Discover expired or outdated content ranking for '[keyword]' and suggest content ideas to replace it."

37. "Provide a list of keywords that are trending but underserved by high-quality content."

38. "Find questions and answers from Google's PAA boxes related to '[topic]' and use them to guide content planning."

39. "Analyze '[topic]' keywords for intent and SERP volatility to identify evergreen vs. trending terms."

40. "Suggest keywords in '[industry]' that are frequently searched on mobile devices with local intent."

💡 Strategy, Funnels & Content Planning

41. "Create a full keyword strategy for launching a new website in the '[niche]' industry with zero authority."

42. "Suggest a keyword-led content plan for building topical authority in '[subject]'."

43. "Design a keyword strategy for increasing product page visibility in a competitive e-commerce niche."

44. "Create a multilingual keyword research plan for expanding a blog to English, German, and Spanish markets."

45. "Generate keywords and matching blog post titles targeting affiliate marketing for '[product category]'."

46. "Build an editorial calendar based on long-tail keywords in '[industry]' sorted by search volume and intent."

47. "Design a keyword strategy for a service-based business that includes blog content, landing pages, and local SEO."

48. "Suggest pillar and cluster content topics using these 3 seed keywords: [keyword1], [keyword2], [keyword3]."

49. "Build a keyword list targeting zero-click searches and provide content tactics to optimize visibility."

50. "Create an SEO content framework using keyword categories for an authority blog in '[your niche]'."

Conclusion: Get Free SEO Consultation

Contact us on Our Website and Get Free Consultation How to Improve Your SEO

Reaching out for personalized SEO assistance can make a significant difference in how your website performs. I encourage you to connect with us at Molly9 Agency (https://molly9.agency), where we understand that every business has unique goals and challenges. Whether you're a webmaster trying to increase traffic, a digital marketeer aiming to boost conversions, or an SEO specialist looking for refined strategies, our team is here to help tailor solutions that resonate with your specific needs. You don't have to navigate the complexities of SEO alone. We're eager to listen to your objectives and provide guidance that fits your vision, ensuring your business gets the focus it deserves.

We pride ourselves on our expertise in SEO and the results we have achieved for our clients. Our approach is not just about general strategies; we delve deeper to understand your industry, your audience, and the unique aspects that differentiate your business. This enables us to create customized SEO plans that are aligned with your goals. From on-page optimization to backlink strategies and beyond, we have the tools and knowledge to enhance your online presence effectively. When you reach out to us, you can expect not only professionalism but also a partnership focused on your success.

As you consider contacting us, remember that improving your SEO is an ongoing journey, and every step counts. Whether you're just starting or looking to refine your existing strategies, having a supportive team can transform your SEO efforts. A practical tip: start by analyzing your current website metrics to identify areas for improvement. This foundational insight will help us tailor our consultation to provide the most relevant solutions, driving your journey toward a more successful online presence.

At molly9.agency We Have More Than 25 Years of Experience

...and We Were Here Since Very SEO Beginnings

Our agency, molly9.agency, prides itself on over 25 years of experience in the rapidly evolving world of SEO and digital marketing. Throughout the years, we've witnessed firsthand the shifts in technology and strategy that have shaped the industry. From the early days of search engines, when keyword stuffing was an acceptable practice, to the sophisticated algorithms we see today that prioritize user experience and quality content, we've been on this journey every step of the way. This extensive background gives us a unique perspective on what works and what doesn't, allowing us to craft innovative strategies that truly resonate with our clients and their audiences. Our hands-on experience means that we've not only adapted to changes but have also thrived amidst them, ensuring our clients stay ahead in a competitive landscape.

Building credibility in the digital space takes time, and our years of expertise have established us as a trusted name among webmasters and digital marketeers. We've collaborated with a diverse array of clients, from small startups to established enterprises, helping them navigate their unique challenges in the digital sphere. This breadth of experience enables us to apply best practices gleaned from various industries while tailoring our approach to fit specific needs. The successes we've achieved for our clients have solidified our reputation as leaders in the SEO space, and we take great pride in being a reliable resource for SEO specialists looking to deepen their understanding and enhance their strategies.

Whether it's optimizing for search engines, creating engaging content, or refining an overall digital marketing strategy, our experience equips us with the knowledge to guide clients confidently. A practical tip for those venturing into SEO is to prioritize quality over quantity in your content strategy. Focus on creating valuable, relevant content that answers the needs of your audience rather than simply chasing traffic with superficial keywords. This approach not only improves your search rankings but also fosters genuine engagement with your audience.

Importance of Good and Honest White Hat SEO Consulting

Reach Out to us For free Consultation Before You Start Your SEO Project

Ethical SEO practices are fundamental to successful digital marketing strategies. When you choose white hat SEO consulting, you are investing in a long-term relationship with search engines and your audience. Ethical practices not only help improve your search rankings but also build trust with users. Search engines are getting smarter, and they prioritize websites that provide genuine, valuable content. By adhering to ethical guidelines, you are ensuring that your website remains both relevant and respected in the eyes of search engines, which ultimately contributes to sustainable growth. A good consultant doesn't just focus on quick wins; they help create a solid foundation for your online presence, guiding you through best practices that align with search engine policies while still achieving your business goals.

If you're planning an SEO project and are unsure where to begin, seeking impartial advice can be incredibly valuable. Many professionals are willing to share their insights without expecting a commitment upfront. This initial consultation can provide you with a clearer understanding of the landscape, helping you make informed decisions. It is also an opportunity to ask questions and clarify what ethical SEO truly entails. Understanding the intricacies of SEO from an expert can set you on the right path and prevent costly mistakes down the road. We offer free consultations that will help you gauge the viability of your plans without any pressure. It's a chance to explore options, gain knowledge, and chart a course that aligns with your ambitions.

Remember that good SEO is not just about ranking higher in search engines; it's about adding value to your audience. A strategic focus on quality content, user experience, and ethical practices will pay dividends in the long run. If you're eager to embark on your SEO journey, starting with honest guidance can make all the difference.

About Author

I am Ivan Bolfek, an SEO consultant from Croatia, and my journey in the digital landscape spans over 25 years. My career started when the internet was still finding its footing; back then, the concept of Search Engine Optimization was in its infancy. I have dedicated my professional life to mastering SEO, digital marketing, and copywriting, and I am currently contributing my expertise at molly9.agency. The evolution of algorithms and online behavior has kept my work both exciting and challenging. Each shift in technology and user expectation has been an opportunity to learn and adapt, allowing me to help businesses improve their online presence effectively.

Throughout my career, I have encountered a multitude of unique challenges and opportunities. Being in this field for so long means I've seen trends come and go, and I've learned that staying current is not just a necessity; it's a responsibility. I regularly engage with other professionals and attend industry conferences to gain insights and share knowledge. One practical tip that has served me well is the habit of continually experimenting with new tactics and technologies. Whether it's testing new keyword strategies or adopting the latest tools for analytics, the willingness to try and learn is crucial. By maintaining an adaptive mindset, webmasters, digital marketers, and SEO specialists can stay ahead in an ever-changing digital arena and better serve their clients.

What do I do

I am passionate about sharing valuable insights and information that empower others to succeed online. Whether you are a business looking to improve your search visibility or an individual seeking guidance on SEO best practices, I am here to help you optimize your online presence.

My mission revolves around education and assistance in the world of SEO. I truly believe that everyone should have access to the strategies and insights needed to improve their online presence. The digital landscape can feel overwhelming, especially with the constant changes and updates in search engine algorithms. Understanding SEO is not just for large corporations; small businesses and individual webmasters can benefit immensely from adopting best practices. It's not just about driving traffic; it's about attracting the right kind of traffic that can convert into loyal customers. By sharing my expertise and insights, I hope to demystify the complexities of SEO and provide others with the tools they need to succeed in this challenging environment.

Taking a personalized approach is crucial when it comes to SEO improvement. I understand that each website is unique, with its own goals, audiences, and challenges. Therefore, cookie-cutter solutions often fall short. Collaborating with webmasters, digital marketers, and SEO specialists means I can tailor strategies that align with specific needs and objectives. Whether it's refining keyword strategies, enhancing on-page content, or building meaningful backlinks, I engage in a consultative process that places emphasis on understanding the individual requirements of my clients. This way, I am not just handing out advice; I am offering targeted action plans for real results. Moreover, staying informed about industry shifts and user behavior is essential, and I strive to guarantee that my advice is always relevant and practical.

For anyone looking to optimize their online presence, one practical tip is to focus on creating high-quality, engaging content that serves the needs of your audience. Rather than merely seeking to achieve higher rankings, aim to provide value through your content. This approach not only improves your SEO but also builds trust with your visitors, increasing the likelihood of conversion. Take the time to understand what your audience is searching for and create content that answers their questions or solves their problems. This simple shift in focus can lead to substantial results over time.